PUERTO RICO
bridge to freedom

PUERTO RICO

bridge to freedom

by EDNA McGUIRE

Foreword by the
HONORABLE LUIS MUNOZ MARIN,
former Governor of Puerto Rico

Illustrated with photographs

THE MACMILLAN COMPANY, NEW YORK

COLLIER-MACMILLAN LIMITED, LONDON

TO JOHN

Whose faith in the ability
of free people to solve
their problems
inspired this book

Library of Congress catalog card number: 63–14000
Fourth Printing, 1967

The Macmillan Company, New York
Collier-Macmillan Canada, Ltd., Toronto, Ontario

Printed in the United States of America

Cover photograph Puerto Rico News Service

*I wish to acknowledge with deep gratitude
the great amount of assistance and
encouragement I received from many people,
particularly during the time I spent
doing research in Puerto Rico.*

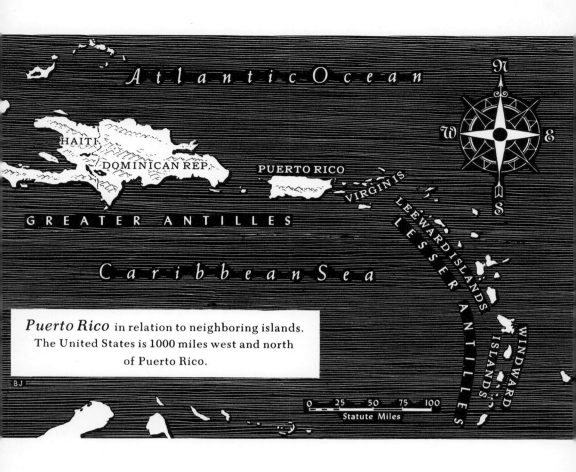

Puerto Rico in relation to neighboring islands.
The United States is 1000 miles west and north
of Puerto Rico.

Foreword

COMMONWEALTH OF PUERTO RICO
LA FORTALEZA, SAN JUAN
OFFICE OF THE GOVERNOR

Dear young friends and readers:

As you will discover when you read *Puerto Rico: Bridge to Freedom* by Edna McGuire, your fellow United States citizens in Puerto Rico are very like you in their passion for liberty and love of democracy.

They differ from you largely in their cultural background. Puerto Rican children learn Spanish at their mothers' knees, are sung to sleep with Spanish lullabies, and—as they grow older—thrill to the cadences of poets like Ruben Darío, García Lorca, and their own Llorens Torres.

At the same time, they are brought up to speak English

as well as Spanish, with the result that Puerto Rico has become the most bilingual place in the Western Hemisphere.

This makes Puerto Rico a particularly exciting place for both North Americans and South Americans to visit and know. In Puerto Rico you can see much that would be familiar in any town in the United States—supermarkets, U. S. movies, baseball games—and much that will be new and stimulating to you, yet which seems familiar to a visitor from Argentina or Mexico.

It is no accident that thousands of visitors come to Puerto Rico every year, not only from Latin America, but also from literally more than one hundred countries throughout the world. Most of them come to study how "Operation Bootstrap" has allowed Puerto Rico to raise its living standards so rapidly, without sacrificing the human values of democracy. It has been said with considerable truth that Puerto Rico has become a sort of working-level United Nations.

We are very proud of this. We are also proud that our close partnership with the United States has proved to be such a fruitful two-way street, beneficial to both. In a world riven by dissension and uneasiness, Puerto Rico's close and harmonious relations with the United States have been one of the brightest spots in the world's rapid evolution toward larger communities, whereby large and small peoples can walk hand in hand in mutual respect, consideration, and dignity.

Luis Muñoz Marín

April 17, 1963

Contents

PART FOUR   *The Commonwealth*

PART ONE

By Way of Introduction

Modern highway connecting Old and New San Juan.

[1]

Winds of Change

Puerto Rico is a land on the move. Planes roar overhead. Cars crowd each other on busy streets and roads. Buses are filled to overflowing with workers going to or from their jobs. School children, laden with books, swarm through the streets. Bulldozers level hillsides. New buildings rise on every hand. Smoke, pouring from tall stacks scattered across the island, tells of mills grinding sugar cane and turning out raw sugar and molasses.

Out of the Past

Yes, Puerto Rico is on the move today, but it was not always so. For more than four hundred years, living conditions changed very slowly. The progress of the island did not keep pace with the needs of the rapidly increasing population. Most of the people lived in great poverty and

San Juan Gate, completed about 1641, the only one of the four original gates in the city walls still standing, leads to a grassy plot overlooking the bay.

with little hope of achieving better conditions. There were not enough jobs for the workers, enough houses for the families, or enough schools for the children.

The Puerto Rican people became desperate. They knew that conditions on their island must change, and they realized that they themselves must bring about the improvements. The changes they set in motion have not solved all their problems. There is still need for more jobs, more houses, and more schools; but the changes have greatly improved living conditions in Puerto Rico. The changes have also given the Puerto Rican people new confidence in themselves. They believe that they can solve other problems, and they are on their way to doing so.

A Bridge to Freedom

The story of the improvements in living that have come to Puerto Rico is an important story for today's world, where so many bloody revolutions are occurring; for the revolution in Puerto Rico has been achieved through the votes of the people, and not by bullets. For more than fifty years, Puerto Rico was under American rule, so the story of the Puerto Rican revolution is of concern to American boys and girls. And this is an exciting story, too; for the Puerto Ricans are showing how an underdeveloped area can change rapidly into a modern, well-developed region. To put this another way, the Puerto Ricans are building a bridge from an old way of life to a new way. It is a bridge over which men may travel from colonialism to the freedom that comes with responsible self-government.

This book tells the story of Puerto Rico. That story, as related here, begins in 1493 when Christopher Columbus discovered the island. It continues with brief mention of major happenings through the centuries. But the story gives greatest emphasis to the recent years, in which Puerto Ricans have been seeking to make their island truly "the Pearl of the Antilles."

[2]

Land of Beauty

Puerto Rico is a green and lovely land, a place of rugged mountains, rolling hills, and fertile plains. The island is actually the crest of a high mountain chain resting on the ocean floor. The mountains run from east to west, with the most rugged area in the central part of the island. The plains lie along the coast, with frequent hills rising from the more level areas.

Puerto Rico is one of the chain of islands that stretches around the Caribbean Sea on the north and east. Together, these islands are called the Antilles. The four larger islands lying to the north of the Caribbean are known as the Greater Antilles; the smaller islands on the east are the Lesser Antilles. Puerto Rico, which is only one hundred miles long and thirty-five miles wide, is the smallest of the Greater Antilles. These islands spreading around the Caribbean Sea are also called the West Indies.

Several small islands near the coast of Puerto Rico are considered to be part of Puerto Rico. The three largest of these small islands are Vieques, Culebra, and Mona. These are sometimes called the Outlying Islands. Vieques and Culebra are east of Puerto Rico, while Mona is to the west.

Puerto Rico is one thousand miles southeast of Miami, Florida; or, as the Puerto Ricans say, "It is only two and one-quarter hours by jet from the States." The Atlantic Ocean pounds the northern coast of Puerto Rico. Its southern shores are washed by the quieter waters of the Caribbean Sea.

Though small in size, Puerto Rico has a population of almost two and one-half million people. This means that, on an average, there are 664 persons to each square mile. But since it is difficult for people to make a living in rugged mountains, the areas where people can live and work more easily are crowded. Land is precious in Puerto Rico and sells for a high price.

San Juan and Other Cities

The largest of Puerto Rico's several cities is San Juan, with a population of almost one-half million. San Juan, located on the north coast of the island, is the oldest city and the capital of Puerto Rico.

The old part of San Juan has narrow streets, some of which are still paved with blue-glazed bricks, brought long ago from Spain. Walls, forts, churches, and government buildings erected several hundred years ago still stand.

The modern section of San Juan has many broad streets and tall buildings. There are stores, banks, hotels, and

factories, much like those found in North American cities. An excellent harbor and a large airport make possible up-to-date transportation for San Juan.

Through the years, the boundaries of San Juan have spread to include near-by smaller cities. However, the names of these smaller cities are still used to locate areas in San Juan. They are also used for postal purposes.

Puerto Rico's second largest city is Ponce, on the south coast. Shipping and manufacturing have made Ponce important. The city has kept many of its early buildings and some of the ways of living followed by early Spanish settlers.

On the west coast is Mayagüez, third in size among Puerto Rican cities. Its good harbor and growing factories are causing it to develop into an industrial center.

A city that has grown very rapidly in recent years is Bayamón, just west of San Juan. Hundreds of new houses, new schools, and big shopping centers are marks of its modern development.

One of the oldest cities in Puerto Rico is Arecibo, on the north central coast. It is in a sugar-producing region and has two large sugar mills near-by.

In the east central part of Puerto Rico, Caguas is located in a fertile mountain valley. It has modern factories, but it has the look of a pleasant, well-kept city of an earlier day.

The second oldest city of the island is San Germán, located in southwestern Puerto Rico. It was founded on the southwest coast, but moved several times. The last move

The tropical foliage on Mona Island, off the west coast, is typical of the luxuriant growth found in most parts of Puerto Rico and the outlying islands.

Philip Hyde

took the settlement to the hills that the city now occupies. Porta Coeli, the oldest church in the Western Hemisphere, is in San Germán. The church is now kept as a museum of religious art.

There are other small cities and towns in Puerto Rico. Many of these are located on the coastal plain, but some are in the rugged interior of the island.

Perpetual Summer

It is always summer in Puerto Rico, for the island lies in the Torrid Zone. But since it also lies in the trade-wind belt, it is never extremely hot. The north and east coasts are cooled by the trade winds by day, and the mountain breezes by night. The southern and western coasts are a little warmer, but the mountain areas are cooler. The average temperatures for the coastal areas are 74 degrees during the winter months, and 80 degrees during the summer months. Rain falls throughout the year, though in less quantity in the southwest, because the mountains reduce the amount of moisture-laden air reaching this area. Except for hurricanes that sometimes blow in with great fury, Puerto Rico has a mild, gentle climate.

Puerto Rico has a parade of blossoms throughout the year. Flowers, bushes, and vines provide a show of striking color, but most vivid of all are the flowering trees. The scarlet and crimson blossoms of the flamboyant trees seem to be in a contest for brilliant color with the orange and scarlet of the African tulip trees. Less gaudy are the orange blooms of the *búcare* and the yellow blossoms of the acacia. Other trees add delicate tones of violet, lavender, and pink to the masses of living color that blanket the landscape.

Philip Hyde

The Rio de la Plata near Comerío flows through a valley in the mountains of east central Puerto Rico.

Many of the forests that once covered the interior of the island have been cut. For years, charcoal was the fuel most used by the Puerto Ricans to cook their food. The forests were cut to provide wood to be made into charcoal.

One original forest that does remain is the Caribbean National Rain Forest, in the northeastern part of the island. The forest is on the side of a mountain peak called *El Yunque* (the Anvil), so it is often called El Yunque Rain Forest. Rain falls in great quantities in this area, so there is a dense growth of trees and giant ferns. Under their shade, delicate orchids, begonias, sultanas, and other flowers bloom. Hummingbirds flit among the trees, and a flock of wild parrots sometimes ventures from the shelter of the forest.

There are very few wild animals in Puerto Rico. However, the mongoose and the iguana are found in certain places, and lizards are common all over the island. The most familiar wild creature, and one that is a favorite of all Puerto Ricans, is a little tree frog called the *coquí*. It takes its name from its shrill cry which can be heard all over the island. "Coqui, coqui, coqui," the little voice cries, all through the night.

Some birds come from North America to spend the winter in Puerto Rico, and others pass over the island while flying from places farther south. But there are birds that live in the island the year around. Among these are thrushes, orioles, grosbeaks, hummingbirds, doves, and owls. A common bird that is a great favorite is the honeycreeper. The Puerto Ricans call this bird the *reinita*, or little queen. It delights in sweets, and will fly through an open window into the house to eat sugar.

Puerto Rico has modern cities crowded with people, but it has not lost its natural beauty. Its mountains still lift their peaks to the blue sky. Its valleys and plains are green with growing plants. Blooming flowers and trees splash color across the landscape. The song of birds and the voice of the *coquí* are heard in the land. In many ways, this island has kept the green and lovely look that it had when seventeen ships came sailing across the Atlantic to land white men for the first time upon its shores.

Mountains overlook a field of sugar cane near Mayagüez.

Philip Hyde

PART TWO

Spanish Colonial Period

The city of San Juan is built around this fine harbor where the Spanish settled in 1508.

[3]

Seventeen Ships A-Sailing

On an autumn day in 1493, seventeen ships set sail from Spain under the command of Christopher Columbus. In 1492 Columbus had discovered unknown islands when he sailed west with three small ships, the *Niña, Pinta,* and *Santa María.* Now called the "Admiral of the Ocean Sea," Columbus set out on his second voyage across the Atlantic Ocean. But instead of the small company that had gone with him the year before, the admiral had fifteen hundred men.

Columbus had left some men on Hispaniola during his first voyage. This island, one of the Greater Antilles, was the goal for his second voyage. But as he sailed up through the Lesser Antilles, he "island-hopped," raising the Spanish flag on one after another of the smaller islands. He found friendly Indians on these islands and put eager questions to them about what lay ahead.

"I Claim This Island"

Always the Indians spoke of a beautiful island called Borinquén. Columbus' heart leaped at the prospect of adding another island to the chain of possessions that he was claiming for the glory of Spain. One November day, his ships came in sight of a green-clad island, and Columbus

The statue of Columbus in Plaza de Colón, at the entrance to Old San Juan, was erected in 1893 on the 400th anniversary of Columbus' discovery of Puerto Rico.

Puerto Rico News Service

knew he had found Borinquén. He sailed along the coast
for a few days, but on November 19 he took a group of men
and went ashore. The "Admiral of the Ocean Sea" stood
straight and tall that autumn day. In solemn voice he
declared, "I claim this island for their Catholic Majesties,
King Ferdinand and Queen Isabella of Spain, and I name it
San Juan Bautista." In English, the name that Columbus
gave to the island means St. John the Baptist.

To this day, no one knows for certain where Columbus
went ashore. Several towns claim the honor of being the
favored place.

The men with Columbus were eager to explore the new-
found island. Their search was rewarded by the discovery
of an Indian village laid out around a central square. They
also found streams of fresh water and filled their water
barrels before they returned to the ships. Among the men
was a soldier named Ponce de León, who liked the look of
the island. When the ships sailed on toward Hispaniola,
Ponce de León gazed back at the green shores with the
hope that he might someday return.

Ponce de León

As the years passed, Ponce de León thought often of the
lovely island. Its beauty haunted him, and he decided
that he must return to San Juan Bautista. Acting on this
decision, he secured permission from the Spanish government to explore and settle the island.

In 1508, with a party of fifty men, Ponce de León landed
on the north coast of the island. The men found a fine
spring, and built their settlement on the shore of a bank

near the spring. They called their settlement *Caparra*. The
settlers had a good supply of water, but they were disappointed to find that the low ground was always damp.
Worse still were the mosquitoes, which thrived in the warm
dampness and made life miserable for the settlers.

Ponce de León found about thirty thousand Indians of
the Arawak tribe living on the island. The Arawaks lived in
villages, each village under its own chief, but with a
principal chief over all the villages. The Arawaks had many
skills. They wove cloth, carved statues of stone, made stone
weapons and tools, and molded pottery. They wére peaceful people, but they often had to defend themselves against
the more savage and warlike Caribs, who lived in the
Lesser Antilles.

Each Arawak man had five or six wives who worked in
the fields, raising tobacco, corn, and ginger. The men
hunted, fished, and rested in hammocks. The Spaniards,
watching the Indians smoking pipes and swinging in
hammocks, decided that here was a way of life worth
copying. Very soon they, too, had pipes and hammocks,
and sometimes Indian wives to wait upon them as well.

The Spaniards discovered some grains of gold in the
streams. Excitement reigned at Caparra. All other activities
stopped while the men searched for the precious metal.
Every settler imagined that he would soon have a fortune,
but the joy was short-lived. The gold gave out, and no
other valuable minerals were found. The men at Caparra
were left with no quicker source of wealth than cultivating
crops on their land. And this presented difficulties, because
farming created a great need for laborers.

Ponce de León was made governor of the island in 1509.

Ponce de León served with Columbus in 1493 when Puerto Rico was discovered, returned in 1508 to found a settlement at Caparra, and became governor of the island in 1509.

The Bettmann Archive

He wanted to treat the Indians fairly, but the pressure for laborers was strong. To the Spanish settlers, it seemed only natural to require the Indians to work for them. The Indians promptly rebelled at this treatment. Spanish soldiers punished the rebels, and even more labor was required. The Indians did not last long at forced labor. Some fled to the mountains and to the off-shore islands. Many died. In time, the Indians disappeared in Puerto Rico as a separate group. Some escaped from the island. Others married Spaniards.

The early loss of the Indians left the Spanish settlers again in need of laborers on their farms. They brought Negroes from Africa to work as slave laborers. The first slaves arrived in 1511. In the years that followed, thousands of Negroes came to Puerto Rico. For three hundred years their labor kept the farms of the island producing crops.

In 1513 Ponce de León sailed away on a new adventure. It is believed that he had heard an Indian story about a magic fountain whose waters restored youth. Legend says that he went in search of this Fountain of Youth. He sailed north and west from Puerto Rico, and one day he came to another land gay with flowers. Ponce de León had discovered Florida.

Later, Ponce was removed as governor of Puerto Rico, and so he decided to return to Florida. On this trip he had a fight with the Indians, and in the fight he was wounded. His men took him to the near-by island of Cuba, where he died. Ponce de León was buried in Cuba. Years later, his grandson carried his remains back to the island he had loved. There they now rest in San Juan Cathedral.

The settlers at Caparra still found their settlement a miserable place to live. In 1521 they decided to move to a small rocky island just off the coast, across the entrance of the bay from Caparra. This bay formed a fine natural harbor, so the new settlement was named *Puerto Rico*. The name means Rich Port or Harbor.

The place chosen for the new settlement was more satisfactory than the site at Caparra. The little island was easier to defend, it provided better dock space for loading and unloading ships, and it was a more comfortable place to live.

For many years, there was confusion in the use of the names San Juan Bautista and Puerto Rico. In time the names as first given were exchanged. The island came to be called Puerto Rico. Its largest city and the capital of the island was called San Juan Bautista, or more briefly, San Juan.

The small green island discovered by Christopher Columbus and settled by Ponce de León grew to be an important Spanish colony. Today, its forts and walls bear silent witness to the value Spain placed upon Puerto Rico as the key to Spanish defenses in the Caribbean.

Ponce de León was buried in San José Church in Old San Juan until 1908, when his remains were removed to San Juan Cathedral.

Commonwealth of Puerto Rico

Key to the Caribbean

Spanish sailing ships sped across the Atlantic, their great white sails full spread. The trade winds blowing from the northeast carried the ships swiftly toward Puerto Rico, which lay directly in their path. How glad the Spanish sailors were to reach this island, their first port of call after the long ocean-crossing! The men knew that fresh water and fresh food awaited them in Puerto Rico.

The Explorers

The Spanish ships brought men of every sort to the New World. There were soldiers, who conquered the native people and defended Spanish claims to land. There were priests, who came to bring the Christian religion to the Indians. There were daring men, who came because they loved adventure. And always there were men who came to seek their fortunes, for treasure was soon discovered in the New World. The Spanish found great stores of gold in Peru, silver in Mexico, and pearls along the shores of Colombia.

These and other riches of the New World were carried back to Spain. Twice each year, a great fleet of Spanish sailing ships came to the Caribbean to gather treasure. The ships scattered to various Spanish ports to take on their cargo. But when they were loaded, the ships once more formed a fleet and sailed together on the homeward journey.

Men sailing under the Spanish flag were the first Europeans to reach the New World. They established Spanish claims both in the Caribbean islands and on the mainland of the Americas before other European nations had sent out explorers. Because of their earlier claims, the Spanish benefited from the riches of the New World sooner than other people. But Spain did not have the rich commerce to herself for long. English, French, and Dutch ships were soon crossing the Atlantic and sailing in Caribbean waters. These ships carried men who came to claim land for the nations sending them out. And some carried men who came to rob the Spanish treasure ships as they sailed home laden with riches.

The Key

Puerto Rico yielded no gold, silver, or pearls with which to load treasure ships, but it played an important part in the duel of nations. Incoming ships took on fresh supplies on the island. Parties were outfitted in Puerto Rico for trips to explore the mainland. The island served as the base from which the Spanish defended their treasure ships. Because of its location, Puerto Rico was the key to the development and defense of Spanish interests in the Caribbean. Its location also made the island an object of interest to other European nations, who tried to seize it for their own advantage.

The Spanish soon came to understand that Puerto Rico had to be held at all costs, both for its value in defending Spanish interests, and to prevent its falling into the hands of an enemy. The building of defenses on the island began early and continued for more than two hundred years.

The Forts

The forts were largely built in San Juan. The harbor there had a narrow mouth that could be guarded. The rocky little island offered a firm base upon which walls and forts could be securely raised.

Visitors today in San Juan go to see the defense structures built long ago by the Spaniards. Many of the forts and walls still stand, silent witnesses of Puerto Rico's contribution to Spanish power in the New World.

In San Juan, a great white house stands on a hill high above the waters of the bay. This is *Casa Blanca,* the house built by the family of Ponce de León. It stands on the tract of land given by the Spanish rulers in recognition of Ponce de León's service. In 1523, after Ponce's death, his son-in-law began building Casa Blanca. When finished, the house served both as a home and as the city's only stronghold.

In later years the house was sold to the Spanish government. Casa Blanca then became the home of the Spanish military commander in Puerto Rico. Today, the commander of the American military forces for the area lives in Casa Blanca. But the outer walls, once the first line of defense for a stronghold, now enclose a charming garden.

The first fort built in Puerto Rico was begun about 1533. It consisted of a tall round tower and a square patio. Later,

Entrance to Casa Blanca, residence of the Commanding General, Antilles Command, and formerly the Ponce family house.

U.S. Army Photo

a second tower was added. The fort, known today as *La Fortaleza* (the Fortress), faced the bay on the western side of the little island upon which San Juan is built. The Dutch burned the fort in 1625, but it was rebuilt later. The fort protected the bay from Carib Indian raids and attacks by pirates, but the Spanish government decided that the location was poor and took steps to build another fort.

It became the custom for the governor of Puerto Rico to live at La Fortaleza, so the fort was changed into a beautiful mansion built around a great central patio. But the old towers still stand facing the bay, reminders of an earlier day. La Fortaleza remains the official residence of the governor of Puerto Rico. It is the oldest house in continuous use as the home of a governor or president in the Western Hemisphere.

The rocky cliff standing at the northwestern end of the little island of San Juan offered a good location for a fort. In 1539 the Spanish began building a fort there. The fort came to be known as *El Morro* (the Headland). For 250 years the Spanish worked on the giant structure, but by 1586 the fort was far enough advanced to permit the first soldiers to occupy it.

El Morro rises 140 feet above the sea. Its great limestone walls enclose storerooms, gun rooms, quarters for soldiers, a prison, a chapel, ramps, passages, and a large courtyard. Beneath it lie huge cisterns to hold the water supply. The fort rises in five levels to the high, windswept ramparts at the top. Cannon once stood along the walls, ready to fire at any attacking ship.

Experience taught the Spaniards that they must protect San Juan from the land as well as the sea. Acting on this

A view from the bay of La Fortaleza, first fort in Puerto Rico and now the residence of the Governor, shows the ancient round towers in the foreground.

idea, they began in 1630 to build a fort on the northeastern part of the island. This structure, which is still standing, is called *San Cristóbal* (St. Christopher). It was the largest fort in San Juan's defense system. San Cristóbal has a large courtyard surrounded by gun rooms, quarters for soldiers, and the other necessary features of a fort. The top gun-platform stands 150 feet above the sea. Five huge cisterns under the fort hold one million gallons of rain water.

Beyond San Cristóbal to the east, the Spaniards built other defense lines and three smaller forts: *Gerónimo*, still standing, *Escambrón*, now only ruins, and *San Antonio*, which was destroyed.

The Spanish built another small fort, *El Cañuelo*, or *San Juan de la Cruz* (St. John of the Cross), across the harbor entrance from El Morro. They also began, in 1630, building walls to extend around San Juan. Work on the walls continued for 150 years. As the city grew, one section of the wall was destroyed, but much of it still stands.

However, only one of the four gates that once pierced the wall is now in place.

El Morro and San Cristóbal were occupied until recent years by military units. Today, these two forts, El Cañuelo, the city walls, and Casa Blanca form the San Juan National Historic Site, under the direction of the National Park Service.

The Spanish built well in Puerto Rico. Their forts stood against enemy attacks, and still stand today, firm and strong.

An aerial view of El Morro, ancient fortress, and Fort Brooke, present-day army post, has the modern city of San Juan in the background.

U.S. Army Photo

[5]

Attacks by Sea and Land

Boom! Boom! Boom! The cannon in El Morro spoke sharply to English ships sailing into San Juan Harbor. Sir Francis Drake, commander of the fleet, expected to surprise the Spaniards on this November day in 1595. He came to capture a Spanish treasure ship in the harbor for repairs. But the gunners in El Morro had keen eyes and a true aim. Their shot tore into Drake's cabin, where he was seated on a stool. As an old account put it, the shot "stroke the stoole from under him" and killed two men.

Drake's guns replied to the cannon in the fort, and the fight was on. For three days the fight raged, with Drake trying to avoid the Spanish fire by moving his ships about. But still the Spanish gunners found their mark. Faced with the choice of flight or the destruction of his fleet, Drake ordered the English ships out of the harbor. El Morro had proved its value as a defense against attacks from the sea.

The English were still determined to seize the island that they recognized as the key to the Caribbean. So, in May 1598, they launched a second attack. George Clifford, Earl of Cumberland, commanded the English forces. Cumberland decided upon a new plan of attack. He landed his forces east of San Juan and marched them overland toward the city.

There had been much sickness on the island, which had reduced the number of men able to defend the city. After two weeks, when food was all but gone, the Spanish defenders surrendered the city to Cumberland. But the same sickness that had weakened the Spaniards attacked the Englishmen. After a few months, it was clear to Cumberland that he could not conquer and hold Puerto Rico. In August he loaded his ships with hides, ginger, and sugar, and sailed away.

Land Defenses

Puerto Rico was still Spanish territory, but the Spaniards now knew that they needed a fort to defend San Juan from attacks by land. Some years later, they began to build San Cristóbal and the outer forts and walls to meet this need.

The Dutch were the next to attack San Juan. In September 1624, a large Dutch fleet, commanded by Boudewijn Hendrikszoon, appeared in the harbor. He called upon the city's defenders to surrender. They refused. He then sent the governor of Puerto Rico a note saying, "Surrender, or I'll burn the city." The governor treated this note with scorn, and Hendrikszoon set fire to San Juan. But the guns of the fort answered fiercely even while the

Sir Francis Drake's fleet puts to sea from English shores in search of Spanish treasure. Drawing by William McDowell.

city was in flames. In the end, the Dutch were forced to sail away to save themselves. The Spaniards rebuilt their burned city, and Spanish rule continued in Puerto Rico.

Two hundred years after Cumberland's attack, the English tried again to seize Puerto Rico. In 1797, Sir Ralph Abercrombie sailed to the Caribbean in command of a fleet. He was sent to take two islands, one of which was Puerto Rico. Abercrombie, with ten thousand men, landed east of San Juan and marched his forces overland. His soldiers made charge after charge against the city's defenses. The attacks went on for a month. Each was met with furious blasts from the guns in the forts. Abercrombie finally concluded that the city could not be taken, and withdrew his forces. Puerto Rico was still a Spanish island.

In addition to attacks by the English and Dutch, Puerto Rico suffered other troubles. For a long period in which France and Spain were often at war, French ships made raids against small coastal towns that had no defense system. One town that felt the fury of the French was San Germán, which had been established in 1512 on the southwest coast of the island. In 1526, a French raid struck a severe blow at the little settlement. Other attacks in later years led the Spaniards to move their settlement away from the coast to the place where the present city of San Germán stands.

Pirates

Pirates anchored their ships in small bays along the Puerto Rican coast, and around the tiny offshore islands. They secured food from the settlers, sometimes paying for it with pirate gold and sometimes not paying at all. They found hiding places for their stolen treasure on these out-of-the-way coasts.

Perhaps the most celebrated pirate haunt was a small island off the south coast of Puerto Rico, not far from Ponce. Legend says that a pirate named Almeida fell in love with a beautiful girl, kidnapped her, and made her his wife. One day Almeida and his pirates fought a battle with the sailors on an English warship. Almeida's wife was killed during the battle. The pirate buried her in a cave on the small island, and since then it has been called Coffins' Island (*Caja de Muertos*).

Many years later another pirate, Roberto Cofresí, ruled

the seas in this area. Probably he found the caves on Caja de Muertos convenient hiding places for the gold and other riches that he stole.

An old story says that Robert Louis Stevenson once visited Caja de Muertos, and that it gave him the idea for the pirate haunt described in *Treasure Island*. Visitors to Coffins' Island sometimes imagine that they hear a faint echo of pirate voices chanting, "Fifteen men on a dead man's chest! Yo, ho, ho! and a bottle of rum!" The flavor of old days lingers on in this tiny island where pirates once waited to pounce upon treasure ships.

[6]

Problems and Progress

The Spanish government believed that all the lands held as Spanish possessions, or colonies, should benefit the mother country. Certain laws were passed to make sure that this was the case.

One such law required Puerto Rico to produce only raw materials. Since the gold was soon exhausted and there were no other minerals of value, this meant that Puerto Rico could produce only agricultural products. Another law required that Puerto Rico trade only with Spain, and that its goods be shipped only in Spanish vessels. Other towns were established in Puerto Rico, but the Spanish rules of trade stated that San Juan was the only legal port. Shipping between San Juan and other towns on the Puerto Rican coast was restricted.

Smuggling and Privateering

The harsh laws concerning trade made it difficult for Puerto Ricans to make reasonable profits. The rules prevented Puerto Rican products from being carried freely from one Caribbean island to another, and even from one Puerto Rican town to another. Because the laws were so severe, smuggling became a common practice. Smugglers carried on trade which was forbidden by the Spanish laws.

Privateering was another practice that developed in the Caribbean. A privateer is a privately armed ship which has permission, from the nation under whose flag it sails, to attack and seize ships or goods of another country. Privateering is no longer practiced, but in the seventeenth and eighteenth centuries many privateers roamed the seas. Puerto Rico became one of the greatest bases in the Western Hemisphere for privateering.

Smuggling and privateering made the Puerto Ricans richer. The trade established by the smugglers created ties of interest between Puerto Rico and other islands in the Caribbean Sea. Similar ties were established between Puerto Rico and the mainland colonies that became the United States. But smuggling and privateering brought evils, too, and Puerto Rican leaders sought to secure from the Spanish government better laws for Puerto Rico.

Better Days

It was a step toward better days in Puerto Rico when the Spanish government granted the island the right to send a representative to the Spanish *Cortes,* or lawmaking body.

In 1810, Ramón Power y Giralt took his seat in the Cortes as Puerto Rico's first representative. Power was an educated man who had served bravely in the Spanish Navy. He lost no time in presenting the problems of the island to the Cortes, and he succeeded in securing improvements in the laws and practices that had prevailed. Within a few years, trade was carried on more freely between Puerto Rico and foreign ports. As a result both agriculture and business in Puerto Rico were benefited.

Puerto Rico made progress in several ways during the nineteenth century. Slavery was ended in 1873. People moved to the island from Spain and other European countries, from the Caribbean islands, South America, and the United States. The sugar crop was increased. New land was planted to coffee. Tobacco continued to be a crop that brought profits to the growers. Some of the Puerto Rican

Luis Muñoz Rivera was the honored leader in the Puerto Rican struggle to secure greater rights of self-government.

Puerto Rico News Service

people gave greater attention than before to art and learning. Writers, musicians, artists, and scientists produced work worthy of praise.

All through this century the Puerto Ricans sought the right to a larger measure of self-government, but they wanted to secure this by peaceful means. An uprising in 1868, instead of growing into a war for independence, ended after only three days. Some leaders in the struggle for more self-government were put into prison or sent out of the island by the Spanish government. But at last there appeared a leader who succeeded.

A New Leader

Luis Muñoz Rivera* came from the mountain town of Barranquitas, where he was born in 1859. He wrote poetry and edited a newspaper that stood squarely against injustice and for reforms in Puerto Rico. Year after year Muñoz Rivera worked to secure greater rights of self-government. In 1897, his efforts were rewarded when Spain granted the Charter of Autonomy. This charter provided for a legislature with some of its members elected by the people. It contained other measures which promised to benefit Puerto Rico.

The Charter of Autonomy was a step forward on the road to self-government for the Puerto Ricans, but it came

---

* The Puerto Ricans often follow the Spanish custom of retaining the mother's family name after the father's name. Thus in the name above, Muñoz was the father's name, Rivera the mother's name. In addressing a person the father's name alone is commonly used. Thus Luis Muñoz Rivera was called Mr. Muñoz.

too late. A few months after the charter was granted, four hundred years of Spanish rule in Puerto Rico ended.

Luis Muñoz Rivera continued, until his death in 1916, to be a man of influence in Puerto Rican affairs. He worked always to secure more rights of self-government for his people. In recognition of this service, he has been called "the George Washington of Puerto Rico."

Today, the home where Muñoz Rivera lived in Barranquitas is a museum. Visitors come to see the desk where he worked, the automobile in which he rode, and other articles that help to create for them the image of the statesman. And they go from the museum to a near-by plot, to stand in silence beside Luis Muñoz Rivera's grave. At the head of the grave sits a carved stone figure of a mourning woman, her head bowed in grief. This figure seems a fitting symbol of Puerto Rico, the motherland, mourning for one of her greatest sons.

Homer Page

PART THREE

American Colonial Period

Luis Muñoz Marín, first governor chosen by the voters of Puerto Rico, speaking at his inauguration in 1949.

[7]

Raising the Stars and Stripes

In 1898, the United States and Spain fought a brief war, which ended in victory for the United States. Clashes between the forces of the two nations took place in Cuba and off Cuban shores. No fighting occurred in Puerto Rico, but it was invaded by American troops and the American navy demonstrated off San Juan. On July 25, 1898, General Nelson A. Miles, with a force of 3,500 men, landed at Guánica, on the south coast of Puerto Rico. The Americans quickly occupied much of the island, and on August 13, the Spanish forces in Puerto Rico surrendered. Most of the Puerto Rican people gave the American troops a warm welcome.

Spanish Colonialism Ends

By terms of the treaty of peace which ended the war, Spain yielded its control of Puerto Rico to the United

General Nelson A. Miles, commander of the American troops, landed at Guánica, Puerto Rico, on July 25, 1898, and occupied the island.

The Bettmann Archive

States. Four hundred years of Spanish colonialism in Puerto Rico was ended on December 10, 1898, and the American flag was raised over the island.

The only value that Puerto Rico had in 1898 for the United States was its location. The island was still the key to the Caribbean, and so could be useful in American defense plans.

There were almost one million people in Puerto Rico in 1898. Most of the people spoke the Spanish language and followed Spanish ways of living.

Despite improvements that had occurred in the nineteenth century, many of the Puerto Ricans were in a sad condition when American rule began. Most of the people were very poor. Many were sick. Malaria, tuberculosis, and diseases affecting the digestive system were common. More than four-fifths of the people could neither read nor write. There were few schools and less than six hundred teachers on the island. Few, other than the sons of wealthy families, had an opportunity to attend school. The Spanish government had wanted all the people to be Catholics, and so had not permitted Protestant churches to be established on the island.

Many Puerto Ricans were poor, but the poorest of all were the *jíbaros,* or country men. They lived on small farms, which they cultivated by such bad methods that their crop yield was small. There were so few roads, especially in the mountains, that the *jíbaros* had difficulty in getting their crops to market. They lived in miserable shacks or in thatched huts known as *bohíos.*

In 1899, a terrible hurricane struck Puerto Rico. The fury of the storm added to the island's misery. Shacks and huts were laid flat. Trees were blown down, and the island's coffee bushes were almost totally destroyed. Thirty-five hundred people were killed.

American Aid

The Americans were concerned about improving conditions of living in Puerto Rico. To this end, the government of the United States set up a public health program. The purposes of the program were to teach people how to prevent disease and to cure those who were ill. Hospitals, medical services, and health education improved conditions, but poverty and ignorance still created health problems.

A public school system was established, with English as the language of instruction. There were not enough trained teachers in Puerto Rico, so for some time teachers from the United States were sent to the island. There was also a lack of school buildings, but as the years went on, more and more schoolhouses were built. In 1903, the University of Puerto Rico was established at Río Piedras, a city that has since become a part of San Juan.

The American people always have had great faith in free public education. They put that faith into practice in Puerto Rico, and the result proved them right. Puerto Rico was able to advance quickly, once progress began, because it had a considerable number of educated citizens. The most successful part of American colonial rule in Puerto Rico was the establishment of schools.

Another important change came under American rule when Puerto Rico was opened to all forms of religion. Several Protestant groups established churches on the island. Some of these Protestant denominations also built hospitals, schools, and children's homes.

Other improvements, begun after 1898, produced benefits shared by many Puerto Ricans. One such improvement was the building of roads. Another was the setting up of a new court system which made justice more certain.

When the United States acquired Puerto Rico in 1898, this nation had had little experience in managing colonies. Congress had to provide a plan of government for the island. Until this could be done, Puerto Rico was placed under military rule.

The Foraker and Jones Acts

Congress passed a law called the Foraker Act, which provided a plan of government. Military rule in the island

Homer Page

The jíbaro, *his face well protected by a* pava, *his hand grasping a tool, knows poverty and hardship.*

ended in May 1900, when the Foraker Act went into effect.

The Foraker Act provided that the Puerto Ricans were not required to pay taxes to support the United States government. Taxes collected on Puerto Rican products shipped into the United States were returned to the treasury of Puerto Rico. Puerto Ricans were given the same rights and protection in matters of trade that citizens of the States had. No corporation could own more than five hundred acres of land in the island. The Puerto Ricans liked all of these features of the Foraker Act.

There were other features of the act that the Puerto Ricans did not like. They were allowed to elect only the members of one house in the legislature. The President of the United States appointed members of the other branch of the legislature, the justices of the supreme court, the governor of Puerto Rico, and the governor's cabinet. The governor was given the power to veto any law passed by the Puerto Rican legislature. The only representative that the Puerto Rican government had in Washington was a resident commissioner. This officer, elected by the people, could sit in the United States House of Representatives and speak on measures affecting the island, but he could not vote on any proposed law.

The Foraker Act did not make the Puerto Rican citizens of the United States. This fact was deeply resented by the Puerto Rican people. They were disappointed, too, because they felt that the Foraker Act gave them less freedom to govern themselves than they had achieved under the Charter of Autonomy.

In 1917, a second law, known as the Jones Act, went into effect. The Jones Act granted United States citizenship to all the citizens of Puerto Rico. The law provided for a senate elected by the Puerto Ricans. This body took the place of the earlier branch of the legislature, the members of which were appointed by the President. But the governor and other officials were still to be appointed by the President, and the governor retained the right to veto the acts of the legislature. Most of the Puerto Rican people were proud of their American citizenship, but they wanted more rights of self-government. They felt that such rights were necessary to solve the problems that troubled them.

[8]

People and Poverty

Economic changes occurred in Puerto Rico during its years as an American colony. Some of the changes produced serious problems.

Sugar

One change was the tremendous growth of sugar production in the island. Americans invested large sums of money to promote the business. Companies were formed which bought great tracts of land, part of which were planted to sugar cane. New sugar mills were built to extract the juice from the cane and make it into raw sugar. The Americans introduced better methods of work both in the fields and in the mills. The effect of these changes was a greatly increased yield of sugar. In 1897, under Spanish rule, Puerto Rico produced seventy thousand tons of sugar;

by 1934, under American rule, the island was producing over one million tons each year.

These gains did not relieve the poverty in Puerto Rico as might have been expected. One reason was that much of the land came to be owned by a few companies. Four of the companies controlled 166,000 acres, or about one-fifth of all the land on the island suitable then for farming. Less than half of the land controlled by the four companies was planted. The rest, held in reserve for future needs, lay idle.

The holding of such large tracts violated the Foraker Act, which stated that no corporation could control more than five hundred acres of land. However, the Foraker Act did not provide a penalty for violating the Five-Hundred-Acre Law. As a result, some owners simply paid no attention to the law.

At certain seasons the production of sugar requires a large number of workers. Harvesting covers about five months. During this period, thousands of men cut the cane, using a heavy knife called a *machete*. Other men haul it to the sugar *centrales*, or mills, where many more workers are employed. When production reached a high level in the American colonial period, more than ninety thousand men were employed in jobs connected with sugar. The difficulty was that most of these men had work for only about five months of the year. During the other months, known in Puerto Rico as the "dead season," they had no way to make a living.

Not all sugar production was in the hands of large American companies. While some Puerto Rican growers sold out to American companies, others continued to produce. A few of the independent growers became wealthy; many did not.

Philip Hyde

In earlier years most of the sugar cane was hauled to the mills on two-wheeled carts drawn by oxen, a method still used occasionally.

The wages of the workers were low, no matter who their employers were. In 1929, a sugar worker's average income amounted to about twelve cents per day for each member of his family. With such wages, many Puerto Ricans had no choice but to be hungry.

As sugar production grew, the raising of other crops dropped. A furious hurricane in 1928 made this situation worse. The hurricane laid banana and citrus groves flat. It destroyed both coffee bushes and the trees that gave them their necessary shade. Coffee production dropped from fifty million pounds per year to five million pounds.

There were few industries in Puerto Rico in Spanish colonial days. That situation did not change much in the first forty years of American rule, but fine needlework was manufactured. To produce the beautiful embroidered garments and linens made in the island, Puerto Rican women sat, day in and day out, bent over their stitching. Their pay was about three cents an hour.

More People, Fewer Jobs

The population of Puerto Rico grew rapidly during the American colonial period. The increase in the number of people, without a sufficient increase in the number of jobs, made poverty worse.

Many country people moved to the cities, where they hoped to earn more than they could in the country. There were not enough houses in the cities to shelter all who came. The people often built small shacks on public land. Thus slums were created in which thousands of people lived crowded together. Growth of trade and increased sugar production had not greatly helped the island's poverty-stricken people. Puerto Rico received the nickname, "poorhouse of the Caribbean."

Some North Americans were disturbed by the poverty and misery in Puerto Rico. One of them was Theodore Roosevelt, Jr., who served as governor of Puerto Rico from 1929 to 1931. In writing of a journey that he took through the hills, Roosevelt mentioned the "lean, underfed women, and sickly men" who had "little food and no opportunity to get more."

Extreme poverty and lack of opportunity produced several results. One was a demand for changes in the ownership of land so that more people could have land. Another was the feeling among the very poor that their future held no hope for better living conditions.

The practice of buying and selling votes was widespread in the island. It was an evil that resulted from poverty and lack of hope. Those who bought votes did it to make certain the election of officials who favored their interests. Those who sold their votes for two dollars each, the going price, did it because the money meant food, or shoes, or some other needed article for their families.

Many Puerto Ricans wanted their island to be granted independence. Some wanted it to become a state of the Union. The poverty and misery that prevailed made stronger the demand for a change in the political relationship of Puerto Rico and the United States.

The Depression

In 1929, a period of great business difficulty began in the United States. Other nations experienced similar business distress at about the same time. This period is often called the Great Depression. It continued well into the 1930's. The effect of the depression was even more severe in Puerto Rico than in the States. People, already desperately poor and hungry, were reduced to near-starvation.

In 1933, an organization, or agency, of the United States government carried out relief measures in Puerto Rico. The agency spent one million dollars a month for Puerto Rican relief. Tons of food were shipped to the island and given to those who were hungry. People were helped to plant home gardens where they might grow food. Women were taught to can the food produced in the gardens. Programs were established to build bridges, schools, hospitals, and other needed public works. Men were given jobs on the public building projects. The relief provided by the federal government eased the misery somewhat during the depression. It did not solve the problems that had created the misery.

PRRA

President Franklin D. Roosevelt and other leaders of government in the 1930's knew that Puerto Rico needed to solve its economic problems. A second government agency, known as the Puerto Rico Reconstruction Administration (also called Relief and Reconstruction Administration), was created. The purpose of the PRRA was to secure improvements in the economic life of Puerto Rico, in order that the Puerto Rican people might have more jobs and broader opportunities to help themselves.

There were bitter differences of opinion about the program of the PRRA. The sugar companies and some other business interests did not believe that the program was wise. They did everything they could to delay or defeat measures proposed by the PRRA. On the other hand, certain Puerto Rican leaders saw the program as a great forward step for the island. The organization operated for several years, most of the time in the midst of arguments about its work.

The attempts to improve the economic life of Puerto

Rico begun by the PRRA provided experience which proved useful in later years. One action of the organization had far-reaching effects. This was the suit filed against a sugar company holding about twelve thousand acres of land, in violation of the Five-Hundred-Acre Law. The case was appealed from one court to another until it reached the United States Supreme Court. In 1940 the court held that the government of Puerto Rico had the right to enforce the Five-Hundred-Acre Law. This decision furnished the basis for a land-reform program carried out in later years.

The efforts to help Puerto Rico during the years of depression made it clear that the federal government alone could not solve Puerto Rico's problems. The Puerto Ricans had to produce a leader who could help them find a solution to their difficulties.

[9]

Year of Decision

On an autumn day in 1940, a crowd of *jíbaros* were gathered in a mountain village in Puerto Rico. In their midst stood a tall, broad-shouldered man. Every eye in the crowd was fixed on the man's face as he pleaded, "Lend me your vote. Don't sell it."

The *jíbaros* considered the man's plea, then heads began to nod in agreement.

"You can't have two dollars and justice," the man continued. "Give us a chance to show you what we can do to help you. All we ask is one chance!"

The Popular Democratic Party

Luis Muñoz Marín was pleading for support from the *jíbaros* for the Popular Democratic Party. He carried his appeal to every town and village and country place in

Puerto Rico. The people listened to his plea. They weighed the question of whether to sell their votes to others, or to lend them to Muñoz and his party. When they voted on Election Day in 1940, they gave their answer. Enough people lent their votes to elect Luis Muñoz Marín to the Senate of Puerto Rico, and to give his party a majority of one vote in the Senate. Puerto Rico had found a leader.

Muñoz Marín was the son of Luis Muñoz Rivera, Puerto Rico's beloved statesman. After Puerto Rico came under American control, Muñoz Rivera had served as resident commissioner in Washington. The son had lived in the United States as a boy and a young man. He had been educated in the States. He had lived and worked as a writer in New York City. Luis Muñoz Marín understood the language and ways of life in the States, but he never lost his deep love for Puerto Rico.

The distress of his homeland drew Muñoz back to the island. He became editor of the newspaper his father had published. He entered politics, and was elected to the Senate of Puerto Rico in 1932. During the depression years, Muñoz worked to improve economic conditions in Puerto Rico. He was looked upon with favor by many people, until he had a serious clash with his own political party, and was dropped as a member.

For a time it seemed that Muñoz had no further political future. But in 1938 he and a few friends organized the Popular Democratic Party. They took as their slogan three words which pointed up Puerto Rico's greatest needs. The words were, "Bread, Land, Liberty." They chose as their emblem a picture of a man wearing the *pava*, or straw hat, widely worn by the *jíbaros*. It was a suitable emblem, for the *jíbaros* believed in Luis Muñoz Marín, and the strength of the new party rested with them.

In the election of 1940, the Popular Democratic Party offered a list of specific measures that they proposed to put into effect if elected. They held a great mass meeting attended by fifteen thousand people. Each of the party's candidates for the Puerto Rican legislature stood up before the crowd and took an oath that he would vote for these measures in the legislature. Muñoz and his friends knew that the appointed governor could veto laws, but they were determined that Puerto Rico should offer a solution to its own problems.

Muñoz had no money. Neither did the new party have funds. But the small sums collected at political meetings or given by faithful friends provided Muñoz with gasoline for his journeys over the island. Day after day, during the campaign, he talked to the people, explaining to them that they could help themselves. He aroused hope in men who had been hopeless in their misery. He gave people faith in their ability to solve Puerto Rico's problems.

Muñoz's plea, "Don't sell your vote," brought victory to the Popular Democratic Party. More important was the fact that vote-buying ceased in Puerto Rico, and honest elections became a habit of the people.

Puerto Rico wanted to be free of colonial rule. The usual path to such freedom is independence. Many Puerto Ricans were ready to follow this path. Most of those who favored independence hoped to achieve it peacefully, by action of the Congress of the United States. These people also hoped that, while granting independence, Congress would at the same time give Puerto Rico certain economic advantages. They understood that, without such favored-nation treatment, Puerto Rico might not survive as an independent country.

The Nationalist Party

A political party, that took the name Nationalist, devoted itself to the cause of independence. The party had a fiery leader, Pedro Albizu Campos, who combined passion for the independence of Puerto Rico with hatred for the United States. In 1932, Albizu ran for senator as a Nationalist, but he received a very small vote. The Nationalist Party received less than 2 per cent of all the votes cast in Puerto Rico in the 1932 election. Since that time, the Nationalists have had no official standing as a political party.

The Nationalists resorted to violence upon several occasions. In the 1930's, a shooting occurred in Puerto Rico. In 1950 the violence extended to the mainland when an attempt was made to shoot President Harry S Truman. Finally, in 1954, four Puerto Ricans stood in the gallery of the United States House of Representatives and started shooting. They wounded five congressmen sitting at their desks in the House.

The violent actions of the Nationalists filled most Puerto Ricans with shame and sorrow. Americans in the States deeply resented the violence, but they realized that the few hatred-filled men and women led by Albizu did not truly represent Puerto Rico. Most of the Puerto Ricans who today favor independence have nothing to do with the few remaining Nationalists.

When Luis Muñoz Marín was a young man, he favored

independence, to be achieved by peaceful means. But in the 1940 campaign, independence was not an issue. Muñoz realized that the poor were less concerned with independence than with relief from poverty. He set out to achieve reforms to relieve the people's misery. He also began to search in his mind for some plan by which Puerto Rico could achieve self-government without losing the advantages it enjoyed while associated with the United States.

The legislature elected in 1940 passed the reform measures pledged by the Popular Democratic Party. The question was whether the governor would sign or veto the bills. The officials of government in Washington sensed the change in Puerto Rican affairs. The bills were signed and a new day had begun in Puerto Rico.

Operation Bootstrap

The program set in motion by the election of 1940 has been called Operation Bootstrap. This was a suitable name because Puerto Rico was, as the old saying goes, "pulling itself up by its own bootstraps."

An important purpose of the reform program was, and still is, to create more industry in order to provide more jobs for people. The program called for buying land owned beyond the five-hundred-acre limit, and distributing part of the land to other owners. Plans were set up to provide more and cheaper electric power. Public housing was built for people living in the slums of the cities. By these and other reform measures, Puerto Rico began to improve the condition of its people.

The program of reform had the support of the governor

of Puerto Rico. In 1941, President Franklin D. Roosevelt appointed Rexford G. Tugwell to this office. Tugwell had been in the island and understood the needs of the people. He had also had experience in affairs of government. He performed a most useful service for Puerto Rico by organizing the machinery of government to run smoothly.

The entrance of the United States into World War II in 1941 brought new difficulties for Puerto Rico. Enemy submarines swarmed in the waters around the island. Supply ships were sunk. Imported food grew scarce. Prices rose. Island products could not be shipped out to market, and this condition threw people out of work. However, the war created a demand for Puerto Rican rum, a drink made from molasses left after raw sugar has been produced from cane juice. The taxes from the sale of rum provided funds with which the Puerto Rican government paid the cost of the new reform program. Considerable numbers of American military men were sent to Puerto Rico during the war. Servicing the military bases provided jobs for many Puerto Ricans who might otherwise have had no work. The payroll for the military men stationed on the island also helped the Puerto Rican economy.

In the election of 1944 the Popular Democratic Party won control of the legislature by a large majority. The party was thus able to continue its program. In 1946, when Rexford G. Tugwell resigned as governor, President Harry S Truman appointed Jesús T. Piñero to the office. Piñero was the first Puerto Rican to serve as governor of the island. His appointment pleased the Puerto Rican people. Piñero supported the reform program, which continued to go forward.

A real advance toward self-government for the Puerto Ricans was assured by an act of the Congress of the United States. In 1947, Congress amended the Jones Act of 1917, to permit the voters of Puerto Rico to elect their governor. The new law also permitted the governor to appoint his cabinet, with the consent of the Puerto Rican Senate.

Luis Muñoz Marín was elected in 1948, the first governor chosen by the voters of Puerto Rico. His inauguration on January 2, 1949, was celebrated joyously in the island. To the Puerto Ricans, it marked a new advance on the march toward self-government.

PART FOUR

The Commonwealth

Today, the flags of Puerto Rico and the United States fly side by side.

[10]

Self-Government at Last

For years, independence or statehood seemed to be the only possible paths to self-government for the Puerto Rican people. But gradually the idea developed that a middle way could be found between these two forms of political organization. And the people accepted the middle way when, on July 25, 1952, Puerto Rico became a Commonwealth. The Puerto Ricans speak of the Commonwealth as "a free associated state." By this, they mean that Puerto Rico is a free, self-governing body of people who are related by ties of common citizenship with the United States.

The Middle Way

The idea of a middle way developed over a period of years. Certain leaders in Puerto Rico and in the United States had suggested some such plan many years before the Commonwealth was established. Luis Muñoz Marín came to believe that this was the proper course for Puerto Rico to follow, and in 1948 the Popular Democratic Party advanced the idea. In 1950, the Resident Commissioner, Antonio Fernós Isern, introduced a bill in Congress which opened the way for developing a Commonwealth. As finally passed, the bill, known as Public Law 600, permitted the Puerto Rican people to vote upon the question of organizing their own government. This law recognized that a compact, or agreement, was to be entered into between Puerto Rico and the United States, if the proposed plan of government was satisfactory to both.

Affairs moved rapidly after the passage of Public Law 600. The Puerto Rican people voted to organize a new government, and they then elected the members of a convention, who wrote a plan of government, or constitution. The Constitution was approved at an election by a large majority of the Puerto Rican voters. Soon afterward, the Congress of the United States gave its approval. On July 25, 1952, the Commonwealth of Puerto Rico was proclaimed.

The announcement of the new "free associated state" was made fifty-four years to the day after General Miles landed with his troops at Guánica. The general had told the Puerto Ricans that he came to bring them the blessings of liberal government, and after fifty-four years the general's words were made real. July 25 is kept as Commonwealth Day, or Constitution Day, in Puerto Rico.

The Constitution of Puerto Rico declares that "the democratic system is fundamental to the life of the Puerto Rican community." It sets up a plan of government which provides for a governor, a legislature, and a system of courts. The bill of rights in the Commonwealth Constitution guarantees Puerto Rican citizens certain rights, or freedoms. Among these rights are equality before the law; trial by jury; freedom of religion, speech, press, and assembly; the right to life, liberty, and the enjoyment of property; and the right to education in free public schools. These and many other guarantees of personal freedom are spelled out clearly in the Commonwealth Constitution.

Because Puerto Rico is associated with the United States, the Puerto Ricans are forbidden by their Constitution from passing any law that is contrary to the Constitution of the United States. For the same reason amendments added to the Puerto Rican Constitution must not be in conflict with the Constitution of the United States.

The Commonwealth of Puerto Rico is in some ways like a state government, and in other ways like an independent republic. But the Commonwealth is neither a state of the Union, nor an independent republic. It is a new form of government created to meet the peculiar needs of the Puerto Ricans. No other government quite like it exists anywhere in the world. The Commonwealth will continue as long as the Puerto Rican people and the government of the United States wish it to be in force, and it can be changed with the consent of both Puerto Rico and the United States.

The Commonwealth uses the system of money and the postal system that operate in the United States. Puerto Rico is protected by the defense forces of the United States, and sends its sons to fight in these armed forces. In all international matters the United States handles Puerto

Rican interests. The Supreme Court of the United States has the final decision in legal disputes in Puerto Rico. In these and certain other ways, Puerto Ricans have the same privileges and responsibilities as other citizens of the United States.

The Puerto Ricans do not vote for President and Vice-President of the United States. But neither do they pay taxes to support the government of the United States. They elect their only representative in Congress, the resident commissioner, who may introduce and discuss bills but may not vote in Congress.

The governor, who is the head of the Commonwealth,

Governor Luis Muñoz Marín speaking to the people of a country district as he sought re-election in 1960. The campaign bus bears the emblem of the Popular Democratic Party.

Newsfeatures Photo

appoints the heads of the departments of the government with the consent of the Senate. The department heads are called secretaries. Luis Muñoz Marín was serving as governor of Puerto Rico when the Commonwealth was established, and was re-elected to the office in 1952, 1956, and 1960.

The Commonwealth legislature, which consists of a senate and a house of representatives, makes the laws. The members of both houses are elected by the people.

The courts provide a means of insuring justice. The Supreme Court of Puerto Rico is the highest court in the island. Its justices are appointed by the governor with the consent of the Puerto Rican Senate.

For purposes of local government, Puerto Rico is divided into seventy-six municipalities. In the municipalities, the people elect the governing bodies and the mayors who serve as heads of the municipal governments. The only exception is San Juan, where the Board of Commissioners, elected by the people, appoints a city manager to serve as the head of the municipal government.

Doña Felisa

The city manager of San Juan is Mrs. Felisa Rincón de Gautier, called simply Doña Felisa by the thousands who love and respect her. Doña Felisa was the oldest of nine children. When her mother died, young Felisa, only eleven years old, became a little mother to her younger brothers and sisters. Today, Doña Felisa mothers all the people of San Juan.

Each Wednesday morning, the city manager holds an

*Doña Felisa Rincón de Gautier listens to a delegation during an
"open house" in City Hall, while other San Juan citizens wait to
speak to her, and observers watch.*

"open house for the people" in City Hall. Hundreds come
each week and wait patiently for a chance to speak to her,
and one by one, or in small groups, they present their
requests. Sometimes the request is for something as important as a house; at other times, it is for something as
small as a pair of shoes or a baseball bat. And often the
request is for help in such matters as rearing a child,
managing a husband, or finding a job.

Doña Felisa listens carefully to each speaker. She cannot
always grant the request, but she can listen. Many persons
whose requests are refused go away comforted, because
Doña Felisa has simply listened and sympathized with
their problems. When a request can be granted, Doña

Felisa signs her name on a slip of paper; and the slip is carried away proudly by the person who made the request, to be presented to the official who will deal with the problem.

When Felisa was a young woman, she was in business in San Juan. She saw the poverty of the people, and decided that they could be helped through political action. In 1932, when women in Puerto Rico were given the right to vote, Felisa was one of the first to take advantage of this new freedom. She was soon drawn into political activity, and in 1938 helped to organize the Popular Democratic Party.

In 1946, Felisa was appointed city manager of San Juan, a position she has held ever since. She works long hours, and gives close attention to the needs of the city. Better housing for her people, clean streets for her city, and nursery schools for the children of working mothers, have been some of her concerns. Each year at the Christmas season, she sees that there are gifts for the children of the poor who lack money to buy gifts. She is never too busy to make visitors to San Juan welcome to her beloved city.

Many honors have come to Felisa Rincón de Gautier. None brings her more satisfaction than the knowledge that her city is well run and her people well cared for. As Doña Felisa puts it, "Being City Manager is just a big housekeeping job."

Elections

Puerto Ricans are interested in politics, and they listen with enthusiasm to the campaign speeches of their favorite candidates. When election day comes, they go to the polls in large numbers to vote. In the election of 1960, 83 per cent of the people who had registered to vote cast their votes on election day.

Through the years, there have been a number of political parties in Puerto Rico, several of which have disappeared. A law requires that a political party must receive at least 10 per cent of the total votes cast in an election in order to offer candidates in the next election. Under the operation of this law, there are at present only two political parties that can offer candidates in the 1964 election, the Popular Democratic and the Statehood Republican parties. However, the law allows a new party, or an old party that receives less than 10 per cent of the votes, to enter an election if they can first present a petition, or request, signed by a sufficient number of citizens. Acting under this feature of the law, other political parties may qualify to enter the 1964 election.

The Popular Democratic Party has the controlling power in the Commonwealth government at present. Governor Muñoz is the guiding influence in this party. The Governor and his party want the Commonwealth to continue as a free, self-governing state permanently associated with the United States. However, Governor Muñoz believes that the compact between Puerto Rico and the United States should be modified to give the Commonwealth certain advantages and more freedom of action in some matters in which its action is now restricted.

Future Status?

The Statehood Republican Party wants Puerto Rico to become a state in the Union. Leaders of this party argue that statehood would give Puerto Rico higher status, or standing, and make its future more secure. They do not regard its position as a commonwealth as being equal in importance to statehood. The movement for statehood has grown stronger since Hawaii and Alaska became states.

Luis Ferré, a leader of the Statehood Republican Party, has been a member of the legislature, and the party's candidate for governor. Ferré is a member of a prominent family in Ponce and a citizen who has given of his time and money to benefit the community. He was educated at the Massachusetts Institute of Technology. He believes that statehood for Puerto Rico will benefit both the island and the United States.

Some Puerto Ricans still strongly favor independence, but their number is much less than in earlier years. In the 1960 election, the Independence Party received only 3 per cent of all the votes cast, thus losing its right, at least for the time being, to offer candidates in the next election.

Symbols of a Free People

The Puerto Rican people are proud of their achievements in self-government. They express their pride through a warm attachment to their symbols of government.

San Juan, the capital city of Puerto Rico, is the home of the beautiful white stone Capitol building. Broad steps lead to the entrance, guarded by eight tall pillars. A big dome rising above the building gives it dignity and meaning. Generous use of white marble adds to the beauty of the Capitol. In the two wings are the meeting rooms of the two houses of the legislature. The Capitol of Puerto

Rico looks somewhat like the Capitol of the United States at Washington, D. C.

The Supreme Court of Puerto Rico meets in its own building near the Capitol. The governor's office, like his home, is at La Fortaleza.

A group of patriotic Puerto Ricans designed a flag while the island was still under Spanish control. The design was for a flag shaped like a rectangle, with one white star on a blue triangular field. Three red and two white stripes completed the banner. A flag with this design is now the official emblem of Puerto Rico, and the white star today stands for the Commonwealth of Puerto Rico.

On July 25, 1952, when the Commonwealth was proclaimed, the flag was raised beside the Stars and Stripes over the Capitol and over all other government buildings. Today, the two flags fly side by side, symbols of the new relationship that exists between Puerto Rico and the United States.

The Seal of Puerto Rico is based upon the rectangular coat of arms given to the island in 1511 by King Ferdinand of Spain. The Seal is a circle, but its symbols are much the same as those on the coat of arms.

The largest figure on the Seal is that of a silver lamb, which is shown on a green field in the center of the Seal. The lamb, said to represent Saint John the Baptist, rests upon a red Bible. The lamb supports the white banner of peace. Under the lamb are the words, "John is his name." The words refer to the fact that the island was first named San Juan Bautista, or St. John the Baptist. The letters F and I, with gold crowns above, stand for King Ferdinand and Queen Isabella, under whose flag Columbus was sailing when he discovered Puerto Rico. Other emblems on the Seal speak of the Spanish past out of which modern Puerto Rico developed.

Hymn

In 1952 the Commonwealth government adopted an official hymn, or anthem. The melody, titled "La Borinqueña," had been known and loved for many years in Puerto Rico, and in other Latin American countries as well. No one can be certain where the melody had its beginning. Felix Astol is generally credited with setting down the music for the first printed copies of "La Borinqueña." The adaptation used in the Hymn of Puerto Rico was made by Ramón Collado. Long after the melody was known, a Puerto Rican poet, Lola Rodríguez de Tío, wrote words to fit it. Mrs. Tío wrote with deep feeling of her native land. The Puerto Ricans have made both melody and words their own. Through the Hymn of Puerto Rico, they express their love for Borinquén, their beautiful island home.

Ways of Living—Old and New

When the Puerto Rican says, *"Esta es su casa,"* "This is your house," he means it. His hospitality towards his guests is generous and freely given, whether his house is a hut or a mansion.

People of several races and many nations have lived in Puerto Rico. Indians, Spaniards and other Europeans, Negroes, Latin Americans, and North Americans have made the island their home. Today, the people of Puerto Rico present a wide variety of appearance. North Americans often think of a Puerto Rican as a slender person with golden-tan coloring and black hair. Actually, skin color ranges from very light to dark, and hair varies from black to blonde. Many Puerto Ricans are short and slender, but some are quite tall.

There is no one set of physical features that describes all Puerto Ricans. But there is one characteristic common to most of them. Puerto Ricans are united in their deep love for their island homeland.

Social Customs

Family life is important in Puerto Rico. The father is respected as the head of the family, in which there are usually several children. But the family circle extends beyond father, mother, and children. It includes grandparents, uncles, aunts, and cousins of every degree. If any member of this large family circle meets difficulties, the other members give him help.

Social life in Puerto Rico is influenced by long-established customs which came to the island from Spain. The towns are usually built around a plaza, or square. In Spanish days, the people often gathered in the plaza when their work was done. In some Puerto Rican towns, this is still the custom on certain days of the week.

At such a gathering, the children dash about the plaza playing games. The men stand in groups, discussing politics and other matters of interest. The women sit on the plaza benches, chatting with neighbors and keeping an eye on the young people who are promenading.

In the promenade, the girls walk in one direction around the plaza, while the boys walk in the other direction. When they meet, the boys and girls glance at each other and smile. A boy, bolder than his mates, may murmer softly to a girl who takes his fancy. And, if the girl likes the boy, the two may then promenade together.

Young unmarried couples in Puerto Rico, who are influenced by Spanish customs, do not go alone to dances or places of entertainment. The mother of the girl, or some other older woman, goes with them.

Another social custom of earlier days, still observed by

some well-to-do families, is the coming-out party. This party, to introduce a girl to grown-up social life, is given by her parents when she is fifteen years old. After she has been introduced with such a party, a girl may attend formal dances and take part in other social activities not open to younger girls.

Spanish became the established language of Puerto Rico while the island was ruled by Spain. It is still spoken by most Puerto Ricans in their homes, and is the language of instruction in the schools. However, English is taught from the first grade through the university, so many Puerto Ricans understand and speak it.

While customs in Puerto Rico often follow Spanish patterns of living, in recent years American customs have also affected island life. Today, Puerto Rico offers a blend of old ways and new ways, of Spanish and American customs. Puerto Ricans carefully preserve old Spanish houses, but they often buy their groceries at a modern supermarket. Puerto Ricans have the Spanish love of poetry and song, but they are wildly enthusiastic about baseball. So it is in many phases of life. The Puerto Rican chooses what he considers to be the best customs of two worlds, and makes these ways his own.

Foods

This mixture of old and new ways affects the habits of eating in the island. The Puerto Ricans' basic food is rice, which is served in various ways, but often with beans or peas. A favorite vegetable is plantain, which grows and looks like a banana. Bread is baked in long loaves that are

*People swim and picnic at Luquillo Beach on the northeastern
coast of Puerto Rico, one of the island's most popular places
for recreation.*

crusty on the outside. Codfish and chicken are eaten
frequently. Desserts are often custards or puddings, though
fried pastries are much enjoyed. Food is more often fried
or boiled than baked, because in early days few homes had
ovens. Modern homes do have ovens, but old food habits
have not been entirely laid aside.

A favorite food for important occasions, such as Christmas dinner, is barbecued pig, known in Spanish as *lechón
asado*. To prepare this dish, the pig is seasoned with salt,
pepper, garlic, and perhaps other herbs. A pole is then
stuck lengthwise through the animal, and it is turned over
an open fire outdoors until it is well done.

The Puerto Ricans enjoy many native foods, but they also like the foods introduced from the States. In recent years, food habits have been influenced by rising incomes. As the Puerto Ricans have earned more money, they have eaten more meat and drunk more milk. With higher incomes, they can afford these more expensive foods. Hamburgers and steaks, served with French-fried potatoes, are now favorite foods in Puerto Rico.

Sports

Puerto Ricans like sports. Cockfighting is one of the favorites there, as it is in other Latin American countries. The fights are held in cockpits during the cockfighting season, which extends from November through August. The cocks are handsome birds with gleaming colored feathers. They are cared for, and trained for the fights, by men skilled in handling them. Men crowd the cockpits to see the fights and to bet on the outcome.

Horses trained to move with smooth strides are exhibited at horse shows. These animals are called *paso-fine*, or fine-step horses. A test of a fine-step horse is for the rider to be able to carry a full glass of water, held high in one hand, around the track without spilling a drop. Horse racing also is enjoyed by Puerto Ricans. *El Commandante*, an excellent race track at San Juan, is the scene of many races.

It is not surprising that water sports have many followers in Puerto Rico. The climate permits swimming, boating, skin-diving, and fishing in all seasons of the year. Deep-sea fishing, especially fishing for blue marlin, is one of Puerto Rico's best-known sports.

Kite-flying was once very popular. The growth of cities and the erection of power lines have cut down the open spaces once used by men and boys for flying kites. Yet the fun has not been entirely lost. When spring rolls around, some kites are still sent flying high, and at least one social club holds a kite-flying tournament each year.

Golf, tennis, basketball, bowling, and other games familiar to North Americans are played in Puerto Rico. There are wrestling and boxing matches, too. But above all other sports, Puerto Ricans like baseball. Almost everybody is a baseball fan, who follows the fortunes of a favorite team. Each of the larger cities has its own team, and these professional teams play through the season, from October to February. At the close of the season, the team that has won the championship of the island plays in the Caribbean Confederation. In this contest, teams from countries around the Caribbean compete for the championship of the Caribbean. The Puerto Rican teams have won the championship several times.

Boys and girls in Puerto Rico have many of the same opportunities that children have in the States. Boys play Little League baseball and are members of Boy Scout troops. Girls may be Girl Scouts. Both may belong to 4-H Clubs. In these clubs, boys and girls carry on projects just as children in the States do.

As in many Latin American countries, a lottery is legal. In a lottery, tickets are sold and a drawing for prizes is held. Puerto Rican lottery tickets sell for twenty-five cents each, with regular drawings once a week. Holders of the lucky tickets receive cash prizes. Four times a year, larger prizes are given in a special drawing. Like all lotteries, only a few of the many ticket-holders get prizes. The others get no return for the money they spent for tickets. The lottery thus yields a considerable sum, which in Puerto Rico goes to charity.

Religion

Spanish settlers in Puerto Rico were Roman Catholics. They brought their religious faith with them and established Roman Catholic churches. As you know, Protestant churches were not allowed in Puerto Rico during the Spanish colonial period, but the Americans granted religious freedom, and a number of Protestant churches were built. The Commonwealth, like the American government, guarantees this freedom to all the people.

The larger part of the Puerto Ricans are still Roman Catholics, but about one-tenth of the people are Protestants. There are also a good many Spiritualists, and some members of the Hebrew faith. The Roman Catholics operate schools, colleges, and a seminary for Roman Catholic priests. Some Protestant churches maintain schools. One of the island's universities began as a Presbyterian school. Several Protestant denominations jointly support a seminary in Río Piedras, now a part of San Juan, where Protestant ministers are trained.

Puerto Ricans in the United States

Puerto Ricans, like Americans on the mainland, move about in search of better jobs. On the island many *jíbaros* move from the country to the cities to find work. Thousands of Puerto Ricans have moved to the States in search of jobs. Many of these people have settled in New York City. Some have gone to other communities.

The Puerto Ricans coming to the mainland often meet difficulties. Some of those who come know little or no English when they arrive. The native Puerto Rican has no idea what winter in a northern country means, and is not prepared for cold weather. Puerto Ricans have little experience at home with racial discrimination. In the States they often meet discrimination, especially in seeking housing. The newly arrived Puerto Ricans are usually compelled, both by lack of income and by racial discrimination, to live in crowded and poor housing. When they find work, they sometimes have to accept lower wages than an employer would pay to a worker born in the States. But despite these and other difficulties that Puerto Ricans meet in the States, they have made useful contributions to American life on the mainland.

The garment industry centered in New York depends greatly upon the quick and skillful fingers of Puerto Ricans. Hotels, restaurants, and hospitals employ many Puerto Ricans and find them satisfactory workers. Farmers in some areas of the country depend upon Puerto Ricans to harvest their crops. In many cases, these agricultural workers come to the States only for the harvest season, returning home when it is finished to work in the sugar-cane harvest.

Puerto Ricans are not confined to any one type of work in the States. They are employed in many industries and trades. Some are well established in business, professions, and sports. José Ferrer and Rita Moreno are Puerto Ricans who are well known on the American stage. Roberto

Clemente and Orlando Cepeda are among the Puerto Ricans who have made outstanding records as big-league baseball players.

Two men who performed great service for the Commonwealth government have been called by President John F. Kennedy to serve the government of the United States. Dr. Arturo Morales Carrión, Deputy Assistant Secretary for Inter-American Affairs in the State Department, deals with matters affecting Latin American countries. Teodoro Moscoso was recently made Co-ordinator for the Alliance for Progress, the program which the United States has established to aid Latin American countries. Moscoso directed the effort to establish new industries in Puerto Rico. Much credit for the success of Operation Bootstrap belongs to him. In his new position, he will work on a similar program for all of Latin America.

In recent years, the number of Puerto Ricans coming to the mainland has dwindled. At the same time, the number returning from the States to make their homes in Puerto Rico has increased. In 1961, more Puerto Ricans returned from the States than went to the mainland. These changes are due to the improved opportunity to find jobs in the island.

The Commonwealth government does not encourage Puerto Ricans to go to the States, but it tries to help those who do go to be better prepared. The people who plan to go are urged to learn English, if they do not speak it, and to improve their job skills. They are advised about weather, housing, and other problems that they will meet in the States. The Commonwealth also has offices in several American cities where there are large numbers of Puerto

Ricans. Through these offices, the Commonwealth government tries to help Puerto Ricans become useful members of the communities in which they live.

The people of Puerto Rico feel the pull between their Spanish past and their American present. They have chosen to keep some Spanish ways and to adopt some American ways. By combining the old and the new they have created a way of living that is neither Spanish nor American, but truly Puerto Rican.

[12]

More Industry, More Jobs

In 1940, Puerto Rico was known as "the poorhouse of the Caribbean." Today, Puerto Rico is the most prosperous island in the Caribbean. The change from poverty to prosperity has been caused in large part by Operation Bootstrap. This program created more jobs for people by setting up industries in the island.

Fomento

In 1942 the government of Puerto Rico formed an organization to promote industrial development. This government agency has grown in importance through the years. Officially named the Economic Development Administration, it is usually called *Fomento*, a Spanish word for development, or promotion.

When the first organization for development of industry

was formed, Teodoro Moscoso was made the head of it. He continued with *Fomento* until recently. As you know, he is now directing the Alliance for Progress for the government of the United States. This is a program intended to help Latin American countries overcome poverty. The program thus deals with problems much like those that *Fomento* met in Puerto Rico.

Teodoro Moscoso was reared in Ponce, where his father owned drug stores. Teodoro attended college in the United States, where he studied pharmacy, returning to Puerto Rico to take a position in the family's business.

When Moscoso became the head of the agency created to bring industry to Puerto Rico, he had no special training or experience for the job. But he had a good mind, he was willing to experiment, and he was devoted to the job he undertook.

World War II was in progress when Moscoso began his work. Since shipping had been hindered by German submarines, Puerto Rico could not get goods that had usually been imported. The new government agency decided to establish factories to produce some of the needed goods.

The war had created a demand for Puerto Rican rum, and the money received from the sale of the rum was greatly needed. But the makers of rum could not get bottles in which to ship their product, so the agency headed by Moscoso set up a factory to make bottles and other glass containers. The agency also operated four other industrial plants. One, a cement plant, was bought by the government. The other three were newly established. In these plants, shoes, clay products, and paperboard for boxes were manufactured.

After five years, Moscoso and his agency made two decisions that affected all later industrial development in Puerto Rico. They decided that factories owned and operated by the government could never provide enough jobs to meet Puerto Rico's needs. This would be true, they realized, because the government would never have as much capital, or money to invest, as would be needed.

The first decision led to the second, which became the basis of *Fomento's* program thereafter. This decision was to use government funds to encourage industries owned by private persons or companies to come to Puerto Rico.

Acting upon the decisions made, the agency sold the five government-owned factories, and was reorganized under its present name, Economic Development Administration. The new program of securing more industry through private investment of money was on its way.

Fomento was concerned with bringing tourists, as well as factories, to Puerto Rico. The climate and natural beauty made the island an ideal place for tourists, but there were few modern hotels. No hotel-owner would take the risk of building a new hotel in Puerto Rico, because the island had no tourists. Teodoro Moscoso believed that one good hotel on the island would start a flow of visitors. *Fomento* built a fine modern hotel in San Juan at the cost of $7,200,000, and leased it to the Hilton Hotel chain. Tourists poured into the new Caribe Hilton Hotel. Other hotels, built with private capital, were soon going up along San Juan's beaches. The tourist business was launched in Puerto Rico.

Fomento organized a plan to attract new industries and new hotels to the island. Companies in the United States were told of the advantages of locating in Puerto Rico.

These advantages include reduced rent on plant buildings, engineering studies, laboratory tests, special training for workers, and other forms of aid. But the biggest advantage offered in Puerto Rico is tax exemption, usually for a period of ten to thirteen years. However, no tax exemption or help is given to a company that closes a plant in the United States in order to open one in Puerto Rico. By holding to this policy, the Puerto Ricans have built up their economy without hurting business in the United States.

Although *Fomento* was the leader in bringing new factories to Puerto Rico, it could not do the job alone. To operate a factory, electricity was needed to supply power. Harbors and ports were necessary in order to ship goods in and out of the island. Roads over which goods could be hauled had to be built. Telephones were needed to speed communication. Schools in which to train workers were needed. These and other needs created by the operation of factories were met by various agencies of government.

New Power

The need for greater sources of power was felt even before the organization to establish industry got under way. During World War II, the lack of sufficient electric power held back military operations in Puerto Rico. At that time, two power systems in the island were operated by a private company, and one system was operated by the government. The Puerto Rican government bought the two private systems and created one system to serve the entire island. Earlier, electric power was generated by use of water going over dams. After the war, when all water resources had been used, and oil could be shipped into Puerto Rico, steam plants were built to generate electricity. Oil was burned to fire the plants.

Today, Puerto Rico has sufficient electric power to turn its factory wheels and light its homes. Power lines run far and wide over the island and are being extended into rugged mountain areas. In such regions, helicopters are used to set the poles and string the wires.

As more industry comes to Puerto Rico, more power will be needed, but the Commonwealth will be ready. A long step toward meeting future needs was taken when nuclear reactors were set up in Puerto Rico. The first such reactor is on the Mayagüez campus of the University of Puerto Rico. It is used to train students in peaceful uses of atomic energy. At the writing of this book, a second reactor was to go into service in 1962 or 1963, and was to supply power to industrial plants in the area of Mayagüez.

Harbors were improved to meet the needs created by increased shipping. A new and much larger airport was built in San Juan in the middle 1950's. In 1961, a huge program to enlarge this airport was begun, though it was already servicing 1,500,000 air passengers each year. San Juan is linked by air service to other Puerto Rican cities and to the Caribbean islands. Jet planes fly on frequent schedules to various cities in North and South America.

The local telephone service in Puerto Rico is being improved. A new underwater cable connecting Puerto Rico and the States has made telephoning between the two places quick and easy.

The Department of Education has helped the industrial development of Puerto Rico in many ways. One specific form of aid has been the training of workers in trade schools so that they will have skills needed in the industries.

The Planning Board

Many agencies and departments of the Commonwealth government have worked to make Operation Bootstrap a success. One agency, the Planning Board, has the responsibility for bringing together in one united effort the work of all the government agencies.

The Planning Board was established in 1942, while Rexford G. Tugwell was governor. The Board has the responsibility for coordinating the work of all the government agencies. The law requires that all building of any type, both public and private, must be approved by the Planning Board. By using its power of approval wisely, the Planning Board has been able to secure orderly development and, at the same time, to provide for future growth.

Fomento's program to establish new industries in Puerto Rico has made satisfactory progress. By September 1962, 769 plants that had been established with the help of *Fomento* were operating in the island. A number of other plants were preparing to open. The plants promoted or helped by *Fomento* were employing more than fifty thousand workers. The Puerto Rican factories produce a wide variety of products which include articles of clothing, textiles, shoes, paper and paperboard, cigars, rubber goods, plastics, metal products, electrical instruments, chemicals, flour, animal food, canned tuna fish, canned pineapples, and cement. A meat-packing plant was recently established to process chickens, hogs, and beef cattle raised on the island. However, the plant has not been in continuous operation. Goods are manufactured both for use on the island and for export. Many articles from Puerto Rican factories are shipped to the States.

The meat-packing plant was built by the government to encourage the production of beef cattle. The action of the government agency in this case was similar to the earlier action in building the Caribe Hilton Hotel. Government funds were used as "risk capital" to start a new productive business, which thereafter used private capital.

Many thousands of visitors arrive in Puerto Rico by plane each year. Other thousands arrive on cruise ships that put in at San Juan for a day or more during a cruise of the Caribbean area. Construction to care for the needs of the visitors continues, as new hotels, longer runways at the San Juan airport, and better docks for cruise ships are being built. There are now good tourist hotels in a number of places in the island. The tourist business provides employment for several thousand Puerto Rican workers. Millions of dollars are spent in Puerto Rico each year by visitors to the island.

Income

Puerto Rican workers have benefited greatly by *Fomento's* program. The workers have had more jobs and their scale of pay has risen. Wages in Puerto Rico are lower than in the United States, but they are better than they were when Operation Bootstrap began. In Puerto Rico the per capita personal income in 1962 was $700 per year. This is more than five times the amount of the personal per capita income in 1940. It is higher than the per capita income in any Latin American country except Venezuela. However, the per capita income in Puerto Rico is still far less than the lowest per capita income of any state in the Union.

Labor unions have grown in numbers and influence since *Fomento*'s program began. The government is sympathetic to the problems of laborers, so certain rights are guaranteed to them in the Commonwealth Constitution. However, the government is opposed to men who try to use laborers and labor unions for their own selfish purposes. The government stands ready to use its influence to prevent such men from entering the labor movement.

A worker operates a machine in one of Puerto Rico's many industrial plants.

Homer Page

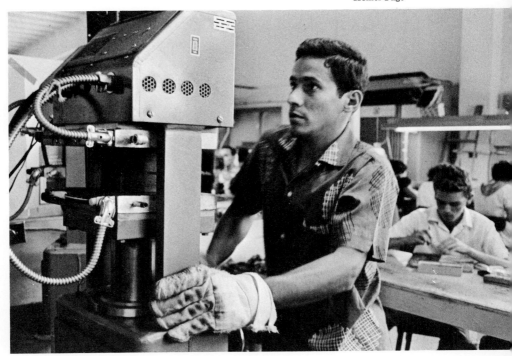

The laborers in Puerto Rican industry have good work records. They usually like their jobs, and they do not often miss work.

There are fewer people now without jobs than in earlier years, but 11 per cent of the workers are still unemployed. New machines, each of which does the work once done by a number of laborers, are being introduced. Each time such a machine is put into operation more people become unemployed.

The future of industry in Puerto Rico is promising. Business is booming. New capital is being invested, and new industrial plants and hotels opened. Incomes are rising. But Puerto Rico dares not rest upon these successes. The population is also growing. The use of labor-saving machines is increasing. The number of unemployed, already too high, will grow larger unless more jobs can be provided. Puerto Rico must push on with its program to provide more industry, more jobs.

[*13*]

A New Look in Agriculture

A wave of rejoicing sweeps across Puerto Rico in late January, for *zafra*, the sugar-cane harvest, is at hand. The long "dead season" is ended for another year. Cane workers sharpen their machetes in preparation for five or six months of cane-cutting.

Sugar Cane

The call for workers goes out when the first fields are ready for the harvest. Early the next morning, the roads are dotted with men answering the call. They come from miles away, many walking, others riding in public taxis or private cars. Hundreds of men pour into the fields where the cane stands thick and tall, higher than a man's head.

By seven o'clock in the morning, a line of cutters forms before the green wall of cane. Swinging their machetes steadily under the blazing sun, the men advance, stripping the blades and cutting the stalks as they move forward. The cane is heavy, but each man levels about five tons in his eight-hour day. When it is finished, the cutter has earned about six dollars.

Sometimes, in the early evening, a cane field is turned into a roaring blaze as it is fired to burn off the blades and undergrowth. The cutters move in early the next morning, while the field is still warm. They are soon grimy from the blackened stalks, but cutting burned fields brings more pay, because the work is dirty.

Here and there, in level fields, a cane-cutting machine moves through the field, doing the work that many machete-swinging cutters would be required to do. There are not yet many cutting machines in use in Puerto Rico, but if their use increases, the island may face problems of greater unemployment, for each machine will throw many men out of work.

The cane is loaded in the fields and hauled to central loading stations, where it is placed on big trucks for the trip to the sugar mill. Most of the loading, once done by men, is now done by machines. Oxen once pulled all the carts that carried the cane from the field. Some oxen are still used, but tractors now pull most of the vehicles that take the cane to the loading stations.

Huge trucks rumble over the roads carrying the cane from loading stations to the mills. There are thirty-two of these mills, or *centrales*, which are spread over the island to serve all the sugar-growing regions.

The trucks stand in line at the *central*, waiting their turn to have the cane weighed and unloaded. A giant lifter places the cane on a moving belt, which carries it to be processed. The cane is cut into small pieces, and large rollers squeeze out the juice, which is then pumped through screens and treated with chemicals to clean it. The juice moves on, through a series of tanks and pans, for other steps in processing which finally produce sugar crystals and molasses. The crystals are raw sugar, which is shipped to refineries to be made ready for the table. The molasses is sold to rum manufacturers.

Sugar cane has been a leading crop in Puerto Rico since the Spanish introduced it in early colonial days. Over the years, it has been the most valuable crop grown in the island.

Tobacco and Coffee

The Indians were growing tobacco when Columbus discovered Puerto Rico. After white men learned to smoke, there was a demand in Europe for tobacco. Settlers in Puerto Rico grew the crop in quantities and shipped tobacco to Spain. Through the years, the growth of tobacco continued in the island. The fields were usually on the mountain slopes or in the hills.

In Puerto Rico, each circle of leaves on the tobacco plant is picked as the leaves are ready. The leaves are threaded together on strings, then hung in tobacco barns to dry, or cure. As each circle of leaves on the plant is ready to pick, the process is repeated. This method of picking and curing requires so much hand-labor that a tobacco farmer's entire family is needed for the work. Children pick the leaves, which the women thread together and the men hang to cure.

For years most of the Puerto Rican tobacco was shipped

Philip Hyde

Tobacco grows on the mountain slopes near Aguas Buenas in east central Puerto Rico.

to the United States. Now there are cigar factories in Puerto Rico. The factories have created an increased need for tobacco. The government encourages both farmers and factories to adopt modern methods of processing the tobacco.

Coffee also is grown in the mountains. The type of coffee favored in Puerto Rico grows under shade trees. Hurricanes in the past have destroyed the trees and the coffee bushes. To help the coffee farmer meet the loss from hurricane damage, the government provides insurance on the coffee crop.

Coffee production in Puerto Rico has risen somewhat in recent years. The government has tried to increase production by setting up a program to aid the coffee farmers. Through this program, the farmers are taught to fertilize and use other methods designed to increase the quality and quantity of coffee. A new type of coffee plant has been tested which grows in the sun and has a greater yield than the shaded type. Farmers are urged to set new plantings of the sun-grown coffee. Some farmers have been sent to coffee-growing countries in South America to learn new methods. By these and other means, the government is seeking to help the coffee farmers to improve their production and their incomes.

Other Crops

Pineapple farming is developing rapidly in Puerto Rico. The government secured a good type of pineapple and produced cuttings for planting by farmers. The production of pineapples created a need for a canning factory, which the government built and operates. Pineapple production has a promising future in Puerto Rico.

Coconuts and bananas of good quality are produced. Grapefruit, oranges, mangoes, avocados, and other tropical fruits can be grown successfully in Puerto Rico. They have not received the attention given other crops, but with care they might become an important addition to the island's agriculture.

At present, there is considerable interest in a native plant long thought to be without value. This is the *acerola,* or West Indian cherry. Tests show that the acerola is very high in vitamin C, the important food element found in oranges and other citrus fruits. Recently a plant has gone into operation to put on the market a food product made from acerola.

Among the crops grown in smaller amounts are plantains, root vegetables, green vegetables, beans, chick peas, and corn. The Puerto Ricans have never grown enough green vegetables for their own needs, but in recent years there has been increasing interest in producing them. Today, growing green vegetables in water, without the use of soil, is being done successfully in Puerto Rico. There are also market gardens growing vegetables to sell. The supermarkets recently opened in Puerto Rico offer a good market for green vegetables, if growers learn to grade and package their products.

Cattle

In recent years, cattle raising has developed rapidly in the island. The government encourages cattle raising by helping farmers develop stronger, healthier animals and better pastures. Puerto Rico now produces almost all the milk used in the island. Some beef is still imported, but more beef cattle are raised each year. Cattle raising was aided by the building of a factory which produces cattle feed, and the construction of a packing plant to process meat. The success of the program to increase cattle raising was shown in 1961–1962, when the income from beef and dairy cattle, plus the income from poultry raising, was one hundred million dollars, which was seven million dollars more than the income from sugar growing.

Land Reform

Agriculture has always been important in Puerto Rico, but certain conditions have hindered its success. The greatest handicap is the small amount of land suitable for farming. Only about one-half of the land in the island can be cultivated, and some of this area has to be treated carefully to prevent loss of soil. The best farmland is in the coastal plains and mountain valleys. Much of the central part of the island is too rugged for farming.

Some increase in the amount of usable land was secured by irrigation. The Commonwealth government has continued a program, which began in the American colonial period, for irrigating land in areas that lacked sufficient rainfall for agriculture.

The practice of landholding in large quantities, which placed much of the island's best land under the control of a few owners, was another serious handicap. This practice began under the Spanish and increased under American colonial rule. In 1940, the Puerto Ricans thought the practice was their most serious problem, and thus it became a major concern of the reform government which was elected in 1940. The enforcement of the Five-Hundred-Acre Law was the first step taken to correct the practice. About one-half the land held by owners, beyond the five-hundred-acre limit, was purchased by the government.

A government agency, the Land Authority, was created.

This agency had the responsibility for carrying out the government's new policies, which were to conserve the island's land and secure the best possible use of it. Acting under this policy, the Land Authority secured for the government certain wastelands and other areas not well suited for cultivation, and planted them to trees and grass. The Land Authority sold part of the government-owned land to some nine hundred landless farmers, on terms of payment that they could meet. The farms thus secured ranged from five to twenty-five acres in size.

The Land Authority did not sell all the government-owned land for small farms, because some crops, particularly sugar cane, the island's leading crop, cannot be profitably grown on small farms. The Land Authority operates much government-owned land in large farms.

A Puerto Rican farmer near Ciales.

Philip Hyde

The practice of one-crop farming, which has prevailed in Puerto Rico since early Spanish colonial days, creates problems. A farmer who grows only one cash crop does not usually produce his own food. The leading cash crops in the island, sugar cane, tobacco, and coffee, are largely exported. Until recent years, almost all the food eaten in Puerto Rico was imported.

Some relief to the difficulties of one-crop farming has been secured as farmers and farm workers have learned to grow food crops and raise livestock. Since one-crop farming is not profitable on a small acreage, the establishment of nine hundred or more farmers on their own small farms has encouraged new farming practices. Farmers have been taught how to fertilize their soil and have been shown good conservation measures. The Land Authority's conservation program has acted to end some of the poor practices that wasted soil.

Agricultural Workers

The condition of farm laborers once presented another serious agricultural problem. These men owned no land. Their wages were so low that they could not provide decent housing or reasonable comforts of living for their families. Many of them were "squatters," living in shacks on land belonging to the companies that owned the big sugar farms. In Puerto Rico, the squatters were called *agregados*.

The reform program that began in 1940 attacked this problem by establishing rural communities where electricity and water were available. Each village was laid out with land set aside to be used for public purposes, such as a school, a store, a health center, a playground, and churches. The land in a village was divided into lots. A lot might be from one-half acre to three acres in size. On it, the *agregado* could raise vegetables, a pig, or some chickens.

The lots were distributed through drawings to the more than fifty thousand *agregados* who qualified. The Commonwealth government continued to own the land, but the *agregados* had the use of it. They were required to put up houses on their lots within four months. Many of them moved the shacks in which they had been living on someone else's land. Few had enough money to build good houses, but the Commonwealth government developed a program to help the *agregados* help each other build better houses. The story of the self-help houses that they built is told in a later chapter.

Some agricultural workers sought to improve their condition by joining labor unions. Between 1900 and 1930, most of the men who worked in the cane fields and sugar mills were organized in local unions. These joined to form a federation which had some established relations with the American Federation of Labor, commonly called the AF of L.

In later years a number of unions and federations were formed in Puerto Rico. In agriculture, only sugar and pineapple workers were organized. Wages and working conditions in these two areas of agriculture were improved. In some types of farming, wages are still very low.

The Commonwealth government pays a small sum to sugar cane workers who can find no employment during the "dead season." The men are encouraged to grow food crops on their small plots of land, to help feed their own families.

The government of the United States and the Commonwealth government both offer aid to Puerto Rican farmers. Their purpose is to encourage farmers to increase production through the use of modern methods and materials. Larger production on each acre is the only way that Puerto Rico can meet the needs of its growing population.

The aid offered to farmers takes many forms and involves many agencies of government. Experiment stations develop new knowledge about plants, animals, methods, and materials. Agricultural and home-economics agents, scattered over the island, help farmers and their wives apply the new knowledge on their own farms. Farmers may borrow money with which to buy seeds, fertilizers, and machinery. They may secure seeds, cuttings, and animals that will raise the quality of farm production. Power lines are extended, and water lines are built to service farm families. Roads are improved so farm products may reach markets. Payments are made, in certain cases, to encourage farmers to follow new practices which will improve production.

Agriculture in Puerto Rico has taken on a new look. Government and farmers have united their efforts to solve the island's long-standing agricultural problems. Some of the problems have been solved. Others present questions to which answers must still be found. Much progress has been made, but there is still much to do.

[14]

A House for Every Family

The people of Puerto Rico have set a goal for themselves. By 1972, they expect to tear down the last shack and have every family on the island living in a decent house.

This is no small task which the Puerto Ricans have undertaken. New houses have been rising for twenty years. Yet, in 1959, a study made by a department of the Commonwealth government suggested that half the people on the island lived in shacks that should be torn down. And in 1962, a housing official stated that probably one hundred thousand people still lived in buildings that did not meet reasonable housing standards.

Homes

Despite the great need for more houses, Puerto Rico does have many good houses. They line city streets and spread over the outlying sections of the cities, where the new housing developments have sprung up. And some of them can be found in rural villages and along country roads.

There are thousands of pretty homes, modest in size, but wearing a well-cared-for and well-loved look. These are the homes of people earning reasonable incomes, who are neither rich nor poor. Not all the middle-income people live in separate dwellings. Many make their homes in apartment houses, which in Puerto Rico are called "condominiums."

The Puerto Ricans are an independent people. They like to own their own homes. Those who live in separate dwellings usually own their houses, and those who live in condominiums own their apartments.

Puerto Rico has some wealthy families, and these people usually have large, handsome houses. Quite often such houses are set in wide grounds and hidden from view by plantings.

The most commonly used building material in Puerto Rico today is concrete. This has taken the place of wood, because concrete stands firm when hurricanes blow, and it is not destroyed by termites. These insects, which are everywhere in the island, eat wood. Occasionally, stone and brick are used for building, but wood is rarely used for new construction.

The modern concrete houses usually have flat roofs. Most of the single dwellings are one story in height. Often they are painted gay colors, and, if there is room, there are usually flowers blooming beside the door. Older houses, and many of the newer ones, have fences around them.

Because the weather is warm all through the year, some houses do not have glass in the windows. If the house is a shack, the window may have only a solid wooden shutter to close against rain or hurricanes. But in better homes, and public buildings, too, windows are often fitted with metal louvered shutters. These shutters have metal slats, or louver boards, that can be turned to admit light and air, or closed to keep out rain.

The very poor people in cities often live crowded together in slums. When industry was first established in cities, the slums grew larger because people looking for work moved to the cities faster than housing could be built. A program called "Urban Renewal" was set up to provide housing for people in the cities. The government agency that directs this program is the Urban Renewal and Housing Corporation. About 65,000 families have used the services of this agency.

In the country, the *bohío* of early days gave place to small wooden shacks. Usually a shack was set several feet above the ground on posts. As you know, part of the program to improve living conditions of farm laborers was the creation of new rural communities. The building of homes in these villages was placed under the direction of an agency in the Department of Agriculture and Commerce, called Social Programs Administration. Today this agency also extends aid in building new houses to small farmers and to communities other than the newly established farm villages.

The Puerto Ricans share in funds provided by Congress to promote better housing in the United States. The Commonwealth government provides the other public funds used in the housing program.

Public housing is built for low-income families by the Puerto Rico Urban Renewal and Housing Corporation, with the aid of federal funds.

Building Their Own Homes

After a group of *agregados* is settled in a new rural community, a man from the Social Programs Administration meets with them. He explains how, by helping each other, the families in the community can have new houses. He tells them the plan for paying for the houses. After the people in the community understand the program, they talk it over among themselves.

When a sufficient number decide to join in the project, a community group is organized. The father of each family is required to give a certain number of hours of labor on the buildings. The agency sends an engineer and a supervisor of construction. With the help of these trained builders, the men of the community put up the houses.

When the program was new, the men completed one house before starting the next. However, this plan was soon changed, and now the men build one step at a time on all the houses. Thus all foundations are put in, one after the other, to be followed by footings, walls, roofs, and floors. Each family in the project takes over its own house when these steps are completed. Doors and windows are installed and the painting is done by members of the family.

The first houses were built of concrete blocks. Now they are made of poured concrete. Each house has three rooms. There is no bathroom in the original house, but a bath is often added as soon as the family can afford it.

A down payment of $25 is required of each family. The cost of the materials for a house was at first $300, then $350. Now the cost is $400, but louvered windows are included at this higher price. Each family pays for its house in ten years by making small monthly payments.

It is a glad day when all the houses in a community project are completed. An official of government comes to make a speech, and quite often in the past that official was Governor Muñoz. The *jíbaros* in their broad-brimmed *pavas* smile and nod as the speaker reminds them of what a great thing they have done for themselves.

After the speeches, comes the high moment of the celebration. One by one, the new home-owners step forward to receive certificates and sign the final contracts for payments. The certificates are accepted with pride and are often hung on the walls of the new houses. There they tell all who look that the man of the house has by his own effort achieved a new position in Puerto Rican life. He has become a home-owner.

Musicians play their guitars and sing of their joy on this day. A great feast is spread and eaten. The musicians begin to coax old, familiar island dance-tunes from their instruments. Soon the whole village is whirling in a dance of sheer happiness.

People in long-established villages often organize self-help building projects. They follow the same plan of work used in the villages established for the *agregados*. It is now necessary for any self-help village project to have at least thirty families taking part.

Self-help houses are also built by the small farmers. Since they do not usually live in villages, the cost is greater and the work goes more slowly, but these, too, are erected by the labor of men who help each other.

Puerto Rico has 16,500 self-help houses spread over the main island and the outlying islands. The program still goes on, so that other countrymen may have clean, strong houses to call their own.

Living in the Cities

Few Puerto Rican cities are entirely free of slums, but because of its size, San Juan has had the greatest slum problem. In the years of great poverty, men who had no place to live threw up tiny shacks on whatever ground they could find. Sometimes they "squatted" on vacant lots, building their poor little shacks in a single night, of packing boxes and scrap lumber. They built quickly and secretly, so that they might be living in the shacks before the owner of the land learned of their presence. They knew that once they were in their shacks, the owner must take legal steps to remove them, and so, for a time, they would have places to live.

Year ago, the squatters began to build on public land along a channel that connects the bay of San Juan with a lagoon, or small lake. When more people pressed into the city searching for jobs, they often added their shacks to the ones already clustered along the channel. Sometimes they drove poles into the water and built out over the channel. Other shacks were scattered in crazy-quilt fashion back from the water, with narrow paths, not fit to be called streets, winding among them. This was *El Fanguito,* "the little mudhole," where fifteen thousand Puerto Ricans once lived in filth and misery.

Another San Juan slum is perched on a hillside, on the tiny island where San Juan began. The shacks elbow each other along narrow paths which run, one above the other, around the hillside. Here in *La Perla,* nine thousand Puerto Ricans live.

As public housing is built, the government moves people out of the slums. Between five and six thousand people have gone out of El Fanguito. But other poor people moving to the city have moved into "the little mudhole." However, there are gains, even in the slums. There are fewer people there than in former times. Garbage is no longer thrown in the footpaths or the channel. Electric lines and water pipes have been extended into the crowded areas.

It is part of Puerto Rico's housing plan to do away with El Fanguito, La Perla, and all the other slums. Most slum-dwellers are happy to find better houses. A few have to be forced to leave. If people cannot be persuaded to move when better houses are available, the government compels them to move. The government holds that it not only should make decent houses available, but also should help people want to live in decent houses.

The first public housing consisted of big apartment buildings set in rows, with playground space for the children. Housing of this type was kept in one area in each city. As the years passed, new plans of building developed. Housing units were built around community centers, with the idea of developing a community spirit among the people living in the units. The new public housing is not confined to any one area within each city, but instead the units are scattered over the city.

Apartment rents in public housing are determined by the size of the family and the amount of the family income. When a family's income becomes large enough for the family to live in private housing, it must move.

The community center in a modern housing unit usually includes a hall for community meetings, a library, a health center, a classroom where women are instructed in better ways to keep house, and a nursery where children of working mothers receive care through the day. A modern housing center may have one housing unit that provides small apartments for old people who live alone. The concern of Puerto Rico for its people reaches from the toddlers in the nursery to the old folks puttering in the "lonely hearts" apartments.

The thirty-five nurseries operating in the San Juan public housing centers are a special concern of Doña Felisa, the city manager of San Juan. She established them to meet the needs of children whose mothers must work away from home. The nurseries are largely supported by the municipality of San Juan.

The children, from two to five years old, are cared for from seven until five o'clock. They have snacks, a hot meal at noon, and naps. They learn to carry on conversations in English as well as in Spanish. They play games, dance, and listen to stories and music. Always they learn safety and health rules, and practice them. More than one mother has said to the nursery teacher, "Now we all wash our hands before we eat, because little Juan says we must."

The small nursery people take part in the celebration of Puerto Rican holidays and festivals. Dressed up in gay costumes, they play their parts with joyful enthusiasm. The costumes are provided by Doña Felisa, and she shares in their merriment on great occasions.

New Programs for Building

In recent years, the Urban Renewal and Housing Corporation has developed a number of new programs. Slum-dwellers do not all go to the public housing centers. Some are helped to buy lots and build their own houses. Some are granted the use of lots upon which they may move their old shacks, if these are good enough. Some are helped to go into housing built by private capital. These various programs are planned to help each family find the kind of housing that best fits its needs and income.

The Urban Renewal program is also seeking to help "the forgotten man." This is the man who has too much income to live in public housing but too little to buy his own house. A new Housing Bank will lend money to such people, and thus help them to become home-owners.

Another purpose of Urban Renewal is to help middle-income families purchase their homes. The agency has erected several small apartment buildings in the past. It is now constructing two fifteen-story condominiums in San Juan. The two condominiums will provide 392 apartments. In all these buildings, the apartments are sold to the families who live in them.

The building of houses with private capital is booming in Puerto Rico. In some cases the Urban Renewal program aids private builders by selling to them, at reasonable cost, public land on which to erect their houses. This makes profits possible for a private builder who is erecting houses to sell, even when the houses are sold at a modest price.

Entire communities of houses built by private capital, using mass-construction methods, have sprung up recently. One such house, of precast concrete, was erected in one hour while Governor Muñoz watched.

The Planning Board has been a powerful force in the battle to provide housing. Through its power to approve all construction, it has helped to direct the efforts of both government agencies and private capital toward a solution of the housing problem. In 1962, the Planning Board, looking toward future needs, proposed that new housing developments should be planned to meet the community and service needs of the people who live in them.

Puerto Rico's goal is a house for every family within ten years. But beyond this goal is another, for the Commonwealth government also aims to lift the lives of its people, to help them live as responsible citizens in the houses that are theirs.

[15]

Basic Rights: Health and Education

The Puerto Ricans believe in the dignity and worth of each person. Governor Muñoz has said that establishing a "sense . . . of the equal dignity and worth of human beings" is one of the great successes of the Commonwealth.

Programs in public health and public education put into practice the belief of the Puerto Ricans. The programs' aims are to secure for the people two basic rights: the right to be healthy and the right to be educated.

Public Health Program

Some of the results achieved by the public health program are startling. Malaria, which once caused three thousand deaths a year, has been wiped out in Puerto Rico. Tuberculosis and diseases of the digestive system, in the past worse killers than malaria, have been sharply reduced. The average length of life was raised from forty-six years in 1940, to seventy-one years in 1960. The death rate dropped to a point lower than the death rate in the States.

When the public health program began in Puerto Rico, many conditions in the island caused sickness. Water was not always pure. There were not enough sewage systems in cities, and almost no means in rural areas to dispose of waste. Many people lacked proper food. There were not enough doctors, nurses, or hospitals to serve the needs of the people.

The health program undertook to attack many health problems at the same time. The wide range of activities employed to secure better health on the island involved a number of government agencies. The combined efforts of the various agencies produced tremendous results.

A pure water supply was provided for both urban and rural areas. Sewage systems were built or extended. Country people were taught to use sanitary methods for disposing of waste. Health instruction was given in the schools, and hot-lunch programs were established for school children. Milk stations, to provide milk for hungry children, were opened. Spraying with DDT, and other measures, were used to rid the island of malaria.

Health centers, dispensaries, and clinics were set up all over the island. Their programs were intended to prevent disease, to teach healthful ways of living, and to give medical care. Hospitals for the more seriously ill were built. Medical and dental schools were established at the University of Puerto Rico. Doctors, dentists, nurses, health teachers, public health workers, and sanitary workers were trained.

All the people who needed medical care were treated. About two-thirds of the people in Puerto Rico received free health service. The Commonwealth Department of Health is now proposing that persons able to pay something for medical service should do so. To put this proposal into effect, each patient's ability to pay would have to be determined by checking his income.

Welfare Services

In Puerto Rico, welfare services are administered by the Department of Health. The Department recently has established a new plan of organization. Under this plan, Puerto Rico is divided into five health-and-welfare districts. Each district will have a medical center with a base hospital. Health centers, operating in all the towns, will each have a small hospital, a public health unit, a bureau to register births and deaths, welfare service, and a station to distribute surplus food.

Under the new plan of organization the dispensaries now scattered over the island will be closed, whenever possible. Persons who were treated at the dispensaries will be taken to hospitals.

The sixty-million-dollar medical center for the northeast district of Puerto Rico is now under construction near San Juan. It includes hospitals specializing in three types of illness, as well as a six-hundred-bed base hospital. This medical center will also serve in the research and teaching program of the University of Puerto Rico's School of Medicine.

All modern medical and welfare services are available in Puerto Rico. The government-operated hospitals give excellent care and treatment. In addition to these, there are a number of private hospitals that also provide good medical service.

The concern of the Commonwealth for the health and welfare of its citizens is shown by the amount of money spent for these services. In 1962, 14 per cent of the Commonwealth budget, or a little more than $44,000,000, was assigned to health and welfare services.

Schools

Boys and girls from the States would find many familiar features if they visited Puerto Rican schools. The buildings, furniture, and classroom equipment are similar to those

A hot lunch, served daily in each of the thirty-five nursery schools maintained in San Juan's public housing projects, contributes to the health of the children.

Puerto Rico Urban Renewal and Housing Corp.

found on the mainland. The schools are organized into elementary, junior high, and senior high schools. Many of the same subjects are taught in American and Puerto Rican schools. There are, however, some differences in the two systems.

In Puerto Rico, the teaching is done in Spanish, which was adopted in 1948 as the language of instruction for all public schools on the island. This decision followed a period of fifty years of changing back and forth between English and Spanish as the basic language in the schools. This period of change created confusion for Puerto Rican children.

Oral English is taught in the primary grades. Above the primary, both oral and written English is taught in all Puerto Rican schools. The English teacher has usually had special training, often on the mainland.

The habit of wearing uniforms in Puerto Rican schools is different from the usual practice in the United States. The girls wear pleated skirts in the school color, and white blouses. The boys wear pants in the school color, and white shirts.

The school term in Puerto Rico is ten months, from August until June. Recently, the schools in one coffee-growing region were operated from February through November. The older children could then pick coffee during the school vacation. This plan was popular with the coffee farmers, and it may be extended to all the coffee-growing areas, but it is doubtful if the boys and girls shared the farmers' enthusiasm for the plan.

Puerto Rico has many children to educate. In 1961, the public schools enrolled 578,338 pupils. The same year found 64,777 pupils attending private schools. A few years ago, many children on the island were not in school, but that is no longer true. In 1961, 90 per cent of all the children of elementary-school age were in school. Even with drop-outs in junior and senior high school, 79 per cent of all young people from six to eighteen years of age were in school.

Puerto Ricans consider education the most important business of government. In 1962, education received 29 per cent of the Commonwealth budget, or some $93,-000,000. This was more than twice the amount spent for health, which received the second-largest share of government funds.

All the public schools on the island are under the direction of the Commonwealth Department of Education. There are also a number of private schools, many of which are operated by churches.

Decade of Education

The years from 1960 to 1970 have been named in Puerto Rico the "Decade of Education." During this period, the Puerto Ricans expect to meet some of their most pressing educational needs.

The first great need is to provide enough classrooms so that every child may attend a full school session each day. At present, almost half the children in the elementary grades attend schools that have two sessions each day. In such schools, half the children attend the morning session, and the other half, the afternoon session. Double sessions are held in both rural and city schools, but there are more of them in rural schools.

The second need is to provide enough teachers so that

teaching loads will be reasonable. Teachers in double-session schools usually teach two groups of pupils, and often the groups are large.

Another need is to secure more and better training for teachers. There are now more than fourteen thousand classroom teachers in Puerto Rico. Some of these teachers have had less than four years of college education. One goal of the Decade of Education is a college degree for every teacher. Present progress suggests that the goal may be reached.

The schools recognize their responsibility to give the students training in more than subject matter. All of the students are expected to develop good standards of conduct. Schools serving the children of families that have lacked opportunities place special stress upon the development of good manners and right habits of living.

The Department of Education has tried to provide each citizen with the type of training that meets his needs. This effort has led to a wide variety of schools and programs.

Many students take vocational courses to prepare themselves for jobs. The Second Unit Rural Schools were established to give country youths vocational training in agriculture and home economics. They operate now as rural junior high schools offering vocational courses. Vocational training is offered to city students in the junior and senior high schools and in twelve special vocational schools. The largest one, the Metropolitan Vocational School in San Juan, can train fifteen thousand students at one time. It offers training in fifty-five trades.

A Hotel School is operated to train hotel workers. This school is carried on with the help of the government agency that seeks to bring tourists to Puerto Rico.

A boys' camp near San Juan takes boys twelve to fifteen years old who have dropped out of school. The boys work, study, and participate in a recreation program. Many of them are persuaded to return to school.

Special programs are arranged for very bright or gifted high-school students. Any such pupil who is too poor to remain in school is given aid so that he may continue his education.

Pupils with musical talent find opportunity in the larger cities to attend the Free Schools of Music. Those in San Juan have the privilege of more advanced training in the High School for Music and the Conservatory of Music. The latter has as its director the famous musician Pablo Casals.

Television and radio are used for teaching purposes in Puerto Rico. WIPR and WIPR-TV are educational stations. They broadcast events of interest, such as music festivals, and offer educational courses. In 1962, a course titled *Let's Learn English* enrolled 5,573 persons. Television sets are sometimes set up in plazas for the use of those who do not have sets in their homes.

The education of adults is a special concern of the Commonwealth. Classes are offered in night school in both English and Spanish. Attention is given to the needs of those who cannot read or write. A special program is provided for war veterans. A variety of vocational courses are open to adults. The success of the adult education program is shown by a rapid increase in literacy since the program began. In Puerto Rico a person is considered to be literate when he can read and write with the ability of a third-grader. About 90 per cent of the Puerto Rican people are literate.

Students in a craft class at Inter-American University at San Germán make block prints.

Books are important aids to education. The Department of Education publishes textbooks prepared to meet the needs of Puerto Rican children. It also sends traveling libraries rolling over island roads to serve 250 communities by lending half a million books.

More than thirty thousand students studied in Puerto Rican colleges and universities in 1962. There are four colleges on the island that offer full college programs. The largest is the University of Puerto Rico, which is supported by Commonwealth funds. The other three schools are privately supported.

The main campus of the University of Puerto Rico is at Río Piedras, now a part of San Juan. The School of Medicine and the School of Dentistry are in San Juan, but not on the Río Piedras campus. On the University's

Mayagüez campus, training is given in agriculture, engineering, and related subjects. The Center for Nuclear Studies is also on the Mayagüez campus. Dr. Jaime Benítez is the chancellor, or head, of the University of Puerto Rico. He is known and respected on the mainland as well as in Puerto Rico.

Fifty years ago John Will Harris, a Presbyterian missionary, started a school for boys in a farmhouse. The small school that he established has grown into Inter-American University at San Germán.

The University of Santa María, commonly called Catholic University, is in Ponce. It has both men and women students. The College of the Sacred Heart is a Catholic school for girls. It is located in Santurce, now a part of San Juan.

There is one private junior college in Puerto Rico. The Department of Education has proposed that five public junior colleges be established.

Community Education

The most unusual educational effort in Puerto Rico is called Community Education. It is a program that reaches far out into the hills and draws the country people into community undertakings. But before there is a community undertaking, the people must feel a need to improve their community.

A man trained to help people in this matter visits the community. He calls upon the families and talks with them about their needs. When the man has come to know the people, he invites them to a community meeting held in the evening. He suggests that those who like to play bring their guitars and other musical instruments.

As the shadows drop over the hills on the appointed evening, the people arrive at the outdoor meeting-place. Everyone comes, some on foot, a few in cars. Babies sleep in their mother's arms. Small children sit quietly, for this is an important occasion.

The musicians in the crowd begin to play, even before all are settled in the folding chairs set up around an electric bulb strung up to light the meeting. The people sing old familiar songs. A few jokes are exchanged. When

all are at ease, the Community Education worker passes out copies of a book. The people look at the picture on the cover and read the title, *El niño y su mundo* ("The Child and His World"). This is one of the books provided, along with films, posters, murals, and other materials, to aid Community Education.

The worker suggests that the book can be read aloud at the meeting. A schoolgirl, glad to show off her ability to

Community needs, and ways of meeting them, are discussed with a Community Education worker.

Homer Page

read, leads off, followed by other young people. The worker puts in a question now and then about the meaning of the book. Little by little, he draws the older people into the discussion. And before the reading is ended, the book has served as a link to lead them to talk of their own community.

When it is time to go home, the worker suggests that each family take a book home to read. He offers to show a film related to the book at another meeting. His offer is quickly accepted, and a date two weeks away is set for the next gathering.

Another discussion follows the showing of the film, and again the people find themselves talking of their own community. At a later meeting, with more community needs suggested, a list is made, and the people decide which problem should be solved first. Often the decision is to build something needed in the community, such as a bridge, road, water line, or milk station. However, projects other than construction are also undertaken. One that has been useful is the holding of classes to teach people to read and write.

In any case, the next step is to consider ways to solve the problem. This often leads to sending a committee to seek help from the mayor or some other municipal officer. If the proposed undertaking involves construction, the committee will ask that a Commonwealth engineer visit the community. When the engineer comes he tells the committee the probable cost of the project and gives advice on the matter. If help cannot be secured from the municipality, the community may send a committee to the Commonwealth agency concerned with their type of problem.

When all information is collected, the community decides in a meeting whether to undertake the project. If the decision is to go forward with the undertaking, a community fund is raised through contributions and money-making events. Labor is volunteered, and, in the case of a construction project, plans are made to borrow necessary machinery from the Commonwealth. When the community has done all it can do, both in raising money and securing volunteer labor, it may apply for help in the form of materials from the Commonwealth. If the project is approved and the materials are provided, work on the project begins.

Months, or even years, after the evening when a book started people to think about their problems, the community undertaking may be finished. By using their own labor and funds, and material and machines provided by the government, the people of the community have solved their problem. At last they have their bridge, or whatever else they needed. They look at the completed undertaking with pride and satisfaction, for it is the creation of their own efforts. With new faith in themselves, they set out to solve the next community problem on their list.

The process has been slow, but the people have learned to work together to solve their own problems. And this is the great lesson that Community Education has to teach.

Fiestas, Festivals, and Fun

Boys and girls in Puerto Rico look forward to fiesta time. Each town on the island has a patron saint, and each patron saint has a special day on the calendar. When their saint's day arrives, the people of a town celebrate with a big fiesta which lasts several days, sometimes for a week or more.

Saint's Day Fiestas

The celebration is held in the town plaza, decorated for the occasion with banners and colored lights. Booths are set up around the plaza. In some booths, fruit-sellers display bananas and other island fruits for sale. In other booths, women cook fried pastries over small charcoal-burning stoves. People sniff the fragrance of the frying food and cluster around the booths to buy the crisp pastries. Eating, laughing, and talking, the people crowd the plaza.

Boys and girls take a spin on the merry-go-round, or make a breath-taking trip aloft on the Ferris wheel, or have a mad swing around the course in a flying boat. On a stage set up for the fiesta, contests are held and programs are given. At intervals a band plays dance music, and dancers fill the plaza.

On the last day of the fiesta, special services are held in the Roman Catholic church. Many people walk in a procession through the streets, carrying an image of the town's patron saint.

The high point of the fiesta comes on the last night of the celebration. Then fireworks are set off with loud bangs, and great splashes of color light the night sky.

The patron saint of San Juan is San Juan Bautista, or St. John the Baptist, whose special day is June 24. The patron-saint celebration lasts for several days and has many features common to all fiestas. But one custom that is different is observed at midnight on June 23. At that time, thousands of people, led by Doña Felisa Rincón de Gautier, crowd the San Juan beaches. At the stroke of midnight, they plunge into the ocean for a swim. Legend says that a midnight swim on this date will keep people young and bring good fortune to the world. The swimmers may not always believe the legend, but they have fun testing the truth of the old story.

A fiesta that draws numerous visitors begins on July 25 at Loíza Aldea. This small village, near San Juan, is the home of many Negroes. The village people celebrate their patron-saint day with some festivities that had their origin in Africa. The visitors come especially to hear the songs and see the dances that come from Africa. But the fiesta at Loíza Aldea is not wholly African, for it also has Spanish elements.

Some patron-saint days are celebrated throughout the island. One such celebration is the fiesta for the Virgin of the Candelaria. This Virgin is the patron saint of Mayagüez, and the fiesta occurs on February 2. However, on this day people all over the island light bonfires. They do this because legend says that the Virgin of the Candelaria protects people from fire.

Christmas Merrymaking

Christmas is a season when Puerto Rican children have the best of two worlds. Like children in the States, they have Christmas trees and gifts brought on Christmas Eve by Santa Claus. But they also keep the old Spanish Christmas customs. One of these is gift-giving on Three Kings' Day, which is January 6.

On the night before Three Kings' Day, children in Puerto Rico put little boxes filled with grass under their beds. The grass is for the camels of the Kings. Legend says that after the camels have eaten the grass, the Three Kings, or the Three Wise Men, as North Americans know them, will leave gifts. Thus it is that Puerto Rican children have the fun and excitement of opening gifts both on December 25 and January 6.

Another Spanish Christmas custom observed in Puerto Rico is the display in the homes of little manger or Nativity scenes. The Nativity groups include Mary, Joseph, the Baby Jesus, the Wise Men, the Shepherds, and the animals.

Carol-singing is a Christmas custom in Puerto Rico.

Groups of people go from house to house, singing old Spanish carols. Musicians, playing guitars and other instruments, go with the singers. In the old days, the singers and musicians were invited into the homes and offered special Christmas food. This custom is still followed in some places, but today people often give them money instead of food.

In Spanish colonial days, children dressed in costumes and went carol-singing. In San Juan they marched first to San José Church, a very old place of worship, each child carrying a basket of fruit or candy. From the church the children went to the Bishop's Palace and the Governor's Palace, singing carols and being treated to refreshments at each place.

During the years of American rule, the people were less careful about keeping the Spanish Christmas customs. Since the Commonwealth was established, Puerto Rican leaders have been concerned with reviving some of the old customs.

A few years ago Doña Felisa, the City Manager of San Juan, invited the children of the city to come, dressed in costumes, to the plaza in front of the City Hall, where a large Nativity scene was set up with live animals. The children came, filling the plaza to overflowing. Some changes have been made since then. Now, during the Christmas season, a Nativity scene stands on a high hill behind Fort San Cristóbal. The plaza has a Santa Claus at one end, and the Three Kings at the other end. Decorated in this way, the plaza serves as a symbol of the Puerto Rican Christmas, combining as it does both Spanish and American customs.

Carol-singing by the children has been encouraged by Mrs. Luis Muñoz Marín, the wife of the Governor of Puerto Rico. Each year Mrs. Muñoz invites the school children to come to La Fortaleza to sing carols. During December the children come, day after day, in large groups. They troop through the courtyard into the great patio of the Palace, where a Nativity scene awaits them. The children come dressed in costumes inspired by the story of the Christ Child's birth. There are shepherds and shepherdesses, Wise Men and innkeepers, Mary and Joseph.

The children sing the old carols beloved by Spanish people through the centuries. And they sing the carols well, for they have learned them in school and practiced them carefully for this great occasion. When the singing is finished, there may be a Christmas play, a Christmas dance, or recitations of Christmas poetry. Each group comes prepared to share in the program.

Mrs. Muñoz smiles and speaks words of praise to the children for their performance. Quite often when the Governor hears the happy voices, he comes down from his second-floor office to the patio to enjoy the Christmas festivity with the children.

After the singing and the program is finished, waiters appear with well-filled trays. In keeping with the old-time custom, the children are treated to Puerto Rican Christmas goodies. Mrs. Muñoz serves *arroz con dulce,* a rice and coconut pudding; *majarete,* rice-flour cream; and *amajábanas,* little fried tidbits made of rice-flour and cheese. The children feast upon the goodies, which for them are the crowning glory of a happy Christmas festivity.

Carnival

Carnival is another gay celebration in Puerto Rico. Balls are given, each of which has a queen dressed in gorgeous costume. There are parades through the streets, music, and dancing.

Carnival normally is held just before Lent begins; but in San Juan, Carnival has been combined with the fiesta for the patron saint. Thus the big celebration in San Juan is in June. However, social clubs still hold balls and choose Carnival queens at the earlier date.

Holy Week and Patriotic Holidays

Holy Week is observed in Puerto Rico with solemn religious ceremonies. The week begins on Palm Sunday with a religious procession through the streets. Both Catholic and Protestant churches hold services on Good Friday. After their service, Catholics often hold a procession in which they carry two figures through the streets. One is a figure of the Virgin Mary, the other the figure of Christ in a glass coffin. Slow, sad music is played during the procession. Joyous services in all the churches on Easter Sunday close the observance of Holy Week.

Puerto Ricans celebrate the patriotic holidays that are observed on the mainland. These include Washington's Birthday, Memorial Day, Independence Day, Discovery or Columbus Day, Veterans' Day, and Thanksgiving Day. They have some holidays, such as Commonwealth or Constitution Day, that celebrate events in their own history.

Weddings, christenings, baptisms, and other personal

events are occasions for family reunions. People able to afford it often belong to social clubs which hold dances and other social affairs. The completion of almost any public project is celebrated with speeches, feasting, and dancing.

Even the working day may sometimes have a bit of festivity. An example from an earlier day was the habit of decorating the oxen that drew the carts on the opening day of the sugar-cane harvest. The long "dead season" was ended. The workers expressed their joy by decking their animals with blossoms.

All in all, there are many occasions in Puerto Rico which provide opportunity for fun. And the Puerto Rican people enter into their celebrations with enthusiasm and joy.

A religious procession passes through the streets of Barranquitas on Good Friday.

Homer Page

[17]

Proud Heritage

A gaily painted truck rolled into the plaza of a Puerto Rican town, followed by a bus. Young men and women piled out of the bus and swarmed upon the truck. Children came running to watch as the young people opened the truck and quickly set up a stage. Young men lifted a painted backdrop into place. Young women put chairs and a bench on the stage.

A watching child clapped his hands and shouted, "A play! A play!" The cry was taken up by the other children who skipped about screaming, "A play! We're going to have a play!"

Doors around the plaza flew open. Heads popped out as people looked to see the reason for the children's noisy joy. When they saw the stage was ready, the older people came to join the children in the plaza.

The stagehands disappeared into truck and bus. By the time the plaza was filled with an eager audience, the young

people had reappeared dressed in costumes. Stagehands
had become actors and the play could begin.

The Theater

The young people who brought the play to the Puerto
Rican town were students in the Drama Department at the
University of Puerto Rico. In their Theater-on-Wheels,
they were taking plays to people far from the university's
campus. The students who took part in the venture did all
the necessary work. They made their own stage-sets, put
the stage and the sets in place, served as actors in the play,
and when the performance ended, packed up the equipment. The Theater-on-Wheels was ready to roll along to
another town.

The traveling theater is only one of several ways by
which Puerto Ricans have an opportunity to enjoy the
theater. Small groups experiment with new plays. Volunteer organizations produce plays for children. Persons
interested in ballet work together to improve themselves,
and sometimes organize children's ballet classes in the
housing centers. The crowning event in the theater arts is
the Theater Festival, held each year since 1958. The
Festival lasts several weeks, and produces plays by Puerto
Rican writers and ballets based upon Puerto Rican folk
stories and legends.

Artists

Puerto Ricans love their little island and the ways of
living together that have developed there. The writers,
painters, musicians, and other artists among the island

people have given expression to the feelings and spirit of the Puerto Ricans. The works produced by these artists and men of learning form a heritage of culture which people today enjoy, and in which they feel pride.

Preserving and adding to the cultural heritage is an important concern in Puerto Rico. Nearly ninety years ago a privately supported organization was formed for this purpose. The organization, *Ateneo Puertorriqueño,* has an active program to encourage many forms of art. In 1955, the Commonwealth government established the Institute of Puerto Rican Culture. The work of the Institute is to preserve and promote all phases of culture in Puerto Rico.

Under the direction of Ricardo E. Alegría, the Institute has carried on a program touching many areas of island life. The Institute is concerned with preserving such records of the past as government papers, books, maps, photographs, paintings, music, and objects of historical or artistic interest. It has charge of museums, parks, monuments, old buildings, and historic places which serve as reminders of Puerto Rico's past. The Institute encourages the production of new works of art through workshops, exhibits, activities such as the theater festival, and scholarships which enable persons gifted in various fields of art to study. In these and other ways, the Institute has built up tremendous interest in the island's culture.

The Love of Music

Music is important to Puerto Ricans. The Spanish influence is greatest in the music of the island, but there are also traces of Indian and African influence.

The guitar is widely played in Puerto Rico. Various styles of this instrument are used, but the six-string Spanish guitar and a four-string instrument called *cuatro* are the most popular. Three instruments that were used by Indians have had a place in Puerto Rican music. These are the drum, the *maracas,* and the *güicharo* or *güiro.* The *maracas* are rattles, often made of round gourds with pebbles or dried seeds inside. A *güicharo* or *güiro* is made of a long gourd, one side of which has been notched. The player scrapes the notched surface with a metal strip. The accordion is favored, especially by carol-singers, in the island.

Old folk songs that were sung for centuries in Spain were brought to Puerto Rico by Spanish settlers. They are still sung in the island, but through the years, changes reflecting Puerto Rican life have crept into the songs. Many of them lived on only on the lips of the singers, who introduced changes as they wished. In recent years, persons concerned with preserving the old folk songs have listened to the singers and made tape recordings. Several forms of the same song are often discovered.

The *aguinaldos,* usually in the form of Spanish Christmas carols, are much loved in the island. Other forms of folk music are the *plena,* combining a lively African rhythm and a Spanish melody, and the *décima.* Both the *plena* and *décima* are made up by the singer to tell a story, and so are similar to ballads. The *décima* has ten-line verses.

The Institute of Puerto Rican Culture holds contests in which each singer makes up a *décima.* The singer is given a line of verse around which his song is to be composed. The song is sung to an old familiar folk tune, and the singer is usually accompanied by musicians playing the guitar, *cuatro,* and *güiro.* There is lively interest in these contests, and the singers are showered with praise.

In the last century, composers of more serious music appeared. They contributed the *danza,* which has ever since been identified with Puerto Rican music. The *danza* is loved because it expresses the mood, or deep feeling, of the Puerto Rican people.

A few years ago, when Pablo Casals was eighty years old, he came to live in Puerto Rico. Casals, a great cellist, was born in Spain, but his mother was a Puerto Rican who often told her son of the beauty of her native island. The coming of Casals was a great aid to the development of serious music in Puerto Rico. He was the guiding spirit in the organization of the Casals Festival, held in San Juan each spring since 1957. Many of the world's best musicians have appeared at the Festival. When Casals was eighty-four, he formed the Puerto Rico Symphony Orchestra, which gives concerts in the principal cities. Casals also established and directs the Puerto Rico Conservatory of Music, where young musicians may receive training.

Painting and Native Crafts

Only one painter of note, José Campeche, appeared in Puerto Rico in colonial days. In recent years there has been increased interest in painting, and also in sculpture and other art forms. The Institute of Puerto Rican Culture displays works of native artists and has sent traveling exhibits of their works to be shown in the States. The Institute and the Community Education Division have given employment to many artists. The posters and murals produced in these agencies have been widely praised for their excellence.

There are several private art galleries in San Juan where artists exhibit their work. In Ponce, Luis A. Ferré opened a museum and gave it to the people of Puerto Rico. This gallery has a good general collection of paintings as well as a room for Puerto Rican art.

There are not many native crafts in Puerto Rico, but the products of one ancient craft survive. These are carved wooden religious figures, known as *santos,* or saints. The original *santos* were carved by men who wanted to express beauty and religious devotion. The *santos* were copied from Spanish religious figures used in churches. But as time went on, the *santeros,* or carvers, made the lines more simple, and changed the figures until a new figure was created.

These santos, *which are excellent examples of an ancient Puerto Rican craft, were presented by Governor and Mrs. Luis Muñoz Marín to President and Mrs. John F. Kennedy.*

Fotografia de La Fortaleza

Carving began early in Spanish colonial days. Today there are no *santeros* left who carve in the old way. The ancient figures carved long ago are nearly all in museums or in the possession of collectors.

The *santeros* often carved a group showing the Three Kings, who play so large a part in the Puerto Rican Christmas celebration. An odd fact about the Three Kings, as shown in Puerto Rico, is that they are always mounted upon horses. The camels, upon which the Kings are often pictured in other countries, seem never to have arrived in Puerto Rico.

Literature

The writing of books was not important in Puerto Rico in early colonial days. There was no printing press in the island until after 1800. During these early years, folk stories and old legends were related by storytellers. Like folk songs, folk stories were often known only in oral form. In recent years, many of these have been preserved by recording them on tape. The stories usually came from Spain, but they underwent many changes as they were told on the island. These changes often brought into the stories mention of places or habits of living in Puerto Rico.

The first book of great worth written by a Puerto Rican was published in 1849. The author, Manuel A. Alonso, called his book *El jíbaro*. A well-known painting, done some sixty years later by Miguel Pou, has the same name. This use of the country man as the subject of story and picture suggests that Puerto Rican writers and artists were exploring their own culture. The *jíbaro* was the central figure on the Puerto Rican scene, and his problems were the problems of the island.

Puerto Ricans delight in poetry. The island has produced excellent verse, much of which has found a place in the memories and hearts of the people.

The Department of Hispanic Studies at the University of Puerto Rico has had a strong influence on the development of good writing in the island. The Department also has created greater pride in the culture of Puerto Rico.

Restoration

The Institute of Puerto Rican Culture is restoring a number of historic places to serve as reminders of the past. An Indian village, in the place where such a village once stood, will recall the life of the island before white men came. Fine old Spanish houses, restored to beauty and usefulness, speak of Spanish colonial days. The home of Luis Muñoz Rivera at Barranquitas is kept as a museum. It houses papers and furnishings, and the automobile that once belonged to the great Puerto Rican leader. The Institute is restoring Fort San Gerónimo in San Juan. This old Spanish stronghold will house a military museum, displaying such objects as models of the Spanish ships that once sailed the Caribbean. A park at Caparra marks the place where Ponce de León established the first settlement in Puerto Rico.

Porta Coeli (Door of Heaven) Church in San Germán is one of the churches established early in the history of the island. Porta Coeli was recently opened as a museum of religious art. The visitor who climbs the high stone steps leading to the old church is rewarded by seeing a finely carved cedar altar and religious figures used long ago in Puerto Rican churches.

La Casa del Libro (The House of the Book), on one of Old San Juan's narrow streets, is an unusual museum, located in a restored house. Beamed ceilings, delicate ironwork, and a pair of patios mark this as a house in the Spanish style. The museum has a collection of more than four thousand rare books. The books are displayed with each exhibit centering around one subject. A recent display showed many different early printings of the story of Don Quixote, the Spanish knight who tried to fight the windmills. The story was published in 1605, and one of the books in the exhibit was printed that year.

The Commonwealth holds that the culture of a country should be shared by all the people. Traveling exhibits, touring concert groups, and the Theater-on-Wheels are all ways to carry culture to the people. But the Commonwealth has a larger plan in the making for accomplishing this purpose. Cultural centers are to be established over the entire island. Already, twenty-six centers are in operation, and it is hoped that in time there will be one in each of the island's municipalities. It is part of the Commonwealth's plan that there will be a building erected at each center which will house a public library and provide a place to carry on such activities as concerts, dance recitals, poetry readings, and art exhibits.

Puerto Ricans accept their culture as a proud heritage from the past. Upon it they hope to build a finer culture in the future.

[18]

Guarding the Peace

Puerto Rico is still important as a base for defense forces. Long ago the Spaniards considered it the key to defending Spanish interests in the Caribbean. When the island became American territory, its greatest value to the United States was its use as part of the national defense system. Today, thousands of men serving in American military forces are stationed in Puerto Rico. They are there to guard the peace by defending both Puerto Rico and the mainland.

Defense Establishments

There are six army establishments in Puerto Rico. These establishments are under the Antilles Command, U. S. Army Caribbean, with headquarters at Fort Brooke in San Juan. The headquarters are housed in a very old building erected in colonial days for religious purposes. The building was completed in 1529.

The officer who heads the Antilles Command lives in Casa Blanca. By using the ancient stronghold as his home, the American commander follows the custom begun by the Spanish, when Casa Blanca was used in colonial days as the home of the commander of the military forces.

The United States Navy has stations in Puerto Rico. The most important of these is U. S. Naval Station, Roosevelt Roads, on the east coast of the island. This base now operates as a guided-missile center. Roosevelt Roads is also the scene each year of special naval exercises. These exercises involve portions of the Atlantic Fleet and sometimes certain foreign navies as well. Vieques and Culebra, the outlying islands off the east coast of Puerto Rico, have naval establishments. The usually quiet life on these small islands becomes exciting when the naval exercises bring activity to their area.

Ramey Air Force Base is located in the northwestern corner of Puerto Rico. It has been a Strategic Air Command base since 1950. This means that planes at Ramey are ready at any hour, day or night, to operate against an enemy who threatens us or our friends.

The presence of the armed services in Puerto Rico contributes to the income of the island. In 1960, the military payroll was $58,000,000.

The United States government provides schools in Puerto Rico for the children of men serving in the armed forces. Children of certain persons employed by the United States in the island may also attend these schools. There are a number of elementary schools and three high schools in this system. The schools are operated under a law passed by the Congress of the United States. They are not a part of the Puerto Rican school system.

The schools for the children of servicemen and U. S. government employees are much like schools in the States. The children study the subjects usually found in mainland schools, but they give more attention to Spanish than is usual in the States. The schools have pleasant buildings, well-trained teachers, modern books, and an active sports program.

Puerto Rican Fighting Men

Puerto Rico has a National Guard which also serves in guarding the peace. The National Guard has seventy-eight hundred members, who form a fighting force that may be called into active duty if the need arises.

Puerto Ricans have proved their loyalty to the United States. More than one hundred thousand Puerto Ricans have served in the armed services of the United States. Some sixty-five thousand of them fought in World War II. Among the servicemen now stationed in the island there are many Puerto Ricans.

The Puerto Ricans made a striking record in the Korean conflict. Records show that 43,434 men from Puerto Rico served in that bloody struggle. A large number of these men volunteered for service. A considerable number of them lost their lives in Korea.

The pride that the Puerto Ricans felt in their fighting men was shown when the 65th Regiment left the island for Korea in 1950. The 65th Regiment, containing thirty-six hundred men, had some American and some Puerto Rican officers. But every man below the rank of officer was a Puerto Rican. At a farewell ceremony in San Juan, the Puerto Ricans, led by Governor Luis Muñoz Marín,

The famous 65th Regiment, shown here on parade, served brilliantly in the Korean War.

expressed their respect and concern for the regiment.

A month later, the men were fighting in Korea and had suffered their first losses. One action quickly followed another. In November, 1950, the Puerto Ricans made sixty-five missions into North Korea to rescue other American fighting men around whom the enemy had thrown troops. The men of the 65th also established a defensive line, to protect American troops being taken out of an area that could not be held. For this service, the 65th Regiment was congratulated, and the commander of the regiment was decorated with the Silver Star for bravery in action.

General Douglas MacArthur, American Commander in Korea, visited the 65th Regiment. In a letter commenting upon the action of the Regiment, he said that these men give "daily testimony of loyalty to the United States. These men are writing a brilliant page with their action on the battlefield, and I am proud to have them under my command."

At the close of the Korean conflict, the colors of the 65th Regiment were returned to Puerto Rico. The colors are kept at the headquarters of the Puerto Rican National Guard in San Juan, where they serve as a reminder of the bravery of the sons of Puerto Rico who served in the famous 65th Regiment.

The Puerto Ricans have proved themselves to be responsible men and good fighters. They stand shoulder to shoulder with other citizens of the United States serving in the nation's military forces. Today, North Americans and Puerto Ricans are united in their decision to defend freedom and to guard the peace of the world.

[19]

A Story to Tell

A native of Ghana moved briskly about a housing center in Puerto Rico. His long gown, blown by island breezes, flapped against his legs as he inspected the community room, nursery, clinic, and library. As each new feature of the center was explained to him by his guide, he nodded his head and exclaimed, "Good! Very good! This we could use!"

A white-robed Nigerian walked through the shops of a trade school, looking closely at its equipment. Later, he put question after question to the head of the school, as he sought information about costs, operation, and training program. He recorded every answer fully for use when he returned to his own country.

A government official from India visited a rural community and took a hand in pouring the concrete foundation for a self-help house. He noted carefully the details of the self-help housing plan, explained by a worker from Social Programs.

A doctor from Panama toured hospitals and rural dispensaries and sought advice from the School of Medicine and the Department of Health. His mission in Puerto Rico was to learn ways by which the health of the people in his country could be improved.

An engineer from Ecuador visited a Puerto Rican dam, to learn how water was used to generate power and help change the life of a region. The man's enthusiasm grew as the inspection continued. Turning to his guide, he exclaimed, "This is the kind of operation that we can use in Ecuador!"

A group of Japanese women, some kimono-clad, visited the island. They represented a consumer's group in Japan and were sent to learn how the interests of the buying public can be protected. The women carried notebooks and wrote down all the information that they gained.

Many Visitors

These visitors to Puerto Rico had heard of the great improvement that had been made in Puerto Rican life. They went to the island to learn how it was accomplished. But the men from Ghana, Nigeria, India, and Ecuador, and the women from Japan were not the only ones who went for this purpose. Since 1950, when the flood of visitors began, 18,955 persons have gone to Puerto Rico to learn how it has started to progress from poverty to prosperity.

These visitors were from more than 125 countries. Many of them were from the new nations that have been created in recent years. Most of these new nations are poor and underdeveloped, but they want to change themselves as quickly as possible into modern, well-developed nations. There are also a number of long-established nations that are underdeveloped. These older nations, too, are now striving to improve their conditions of living.

Puerto Rico has a story to tell to all underdeveloped countries. It is the story of how the Puerto Ricans are lifting themselves from poverty and misery to modern standards of living. But it is also the story of how this is being accomplished under a free, democratic government. In some underdeveloped countries, leaders have seized power that properly belongs to the people. Their excuse for such action is that their nations can develop more rapidly if a strong man, or dictator, heads the government.

Puerto Rico stands as the shining example of a country that has both progress and freedom. For this reason it is sometimes called "a showcase of democracy."

Puerto Rico as a Laboratory

In a sense, Puerto Rico has become a laboratory in which the people test new ways of meeting old problems. The visitors who come from other nations enter the laboratory to observe the experiment and its results.

Puerto Rico's service as a laboratory began with a speech by Harry S Truman. When President Truman took office as President in 1949, he included, as Point Four in his inaugural address, a new idea. The President proposed that the United States make available to under-developed countries the results of our scientific and industrial progress.

Governor Muñoz visited President Truman soon after the address was given. The Governor told the President that Puerto Rico, in its Operation Bootstrap, was applying the results of scientific and industrial knowledge to the solution of its problems. He said that the Puerto Ricans would gladly teach others what they had learned by experience. The President accepted this offer.

At the Governor's request, the legislature appropriated funds to support a program which would enable Puerto Rico to share its knowledge with underdeveloped countries. This was the first money appropriated to support what came to be called the Point Four Program. Later the Congress of the United States also provided funds for the program. The Puerto Rican legislature has continued to provide new funds each year to support the work of teaching skills needed in developing a country.

In May 1950, fifteen engineers from Latin American countries arrived in Puerto Rico. They came to study the plan by which the Commonwealth's water and power development had been achieved. These were the first of the thousands of visitors who have come to Puerto Rico from underdeveloped countries.

Puerto Rico is well fitted to serve as a laboratory for the visitors. The situations that exist in the island are found in many underdeveloped countries, thus allowing visitors to profit by the experience of the Puerto Ricans. The work of solving many of Puerto Rico's problems is far enough advanced to show three stages. Visitors to the island can see: (1) a problem still existing in some areas, (2) the process of solving the problem in operation in other areas, and (3) the results of the problem's having been solved in still other areas.

Puerto Rico's size is helpful to those who come to learn, because they can more easily understand an operation on a small scale. They do not feel overcome by "bigness," as foreign observers sometimes do in the States. Since many underdeveloped nations are small, Puerto Rican methods that operate on a small scale are often well fitted to their needs.

The rate of development has been very rapid in Puerto Rico, yet this rate has been achieved with a government that is elected by the people. This situation presents the best possible answer to those foreign leaders who think that the rate of growth can be rapid only in a country ruled by a dictator.

Puerto Rico has used the principle of self-help to solve some of its problems. The underdeveloped countries usually are poor. The principle of self-help offers them a plan for meeting such needs as housing and roads.

Many Latin Americans come to Puerto Rico to study in its colleges and to observe new methods of work. They find the island well suited to their purposes because Spanish, which they also speak, is its basic language.

The Learners

The people who come to learn of Puerto Rico's program of development fall into three groups. Persons in the first group come to learn specific techniques, or ways to work. In this group are the people who want to learn how to build houses, roads, water systems, power plants, and other forms of construction. This group also includes those who want to establish and operate industries and business concerns, and administer departments of government. These and all others seeking to learn new techniques are placed in Puerto Rico's Technical Co-operation Program. As a matter of convenience these people are called "trainees." The Latin American engineers, who came in May 1950, might be considered the first trainees. Between the date of their coming and the end of 1961, 9,425 trainees took part in the Technical Co-operation Program.

A second group comes to observe Puerto Rico's educational, cultural, economic, and political life. Among these people, known as "observers," are teachers, journalists, writers, officials of government, and other people who influence opinion in their homelands. In Puerto Rico the observers are in the Educational Exchange Program. Since observers began to come, 3,118 of them have viewed life in Puerto Rico.

From time to time, meetings to study certain specific problems are held in Puerto Rico. By the end of 1961, these meetings had brought 4,042 visitors from other countries to the island. These people make up the third group who come to learn of Puerto Rico's development.

Trainees, observers, and visitors have come from widely scattered parts of the world, but about half of them came from Latin America. The small nations in the Caribbean area sent about one-seventh of the total group. An equally large number came from the Far East. Included in this group were men and women from the island nations, Indonesia and the Philippines, as well as others from eastern Asia. Western and southern Asia and Africa supplied a considerable number. Three well-developed areas, Europe, Canada, and the United States, were also

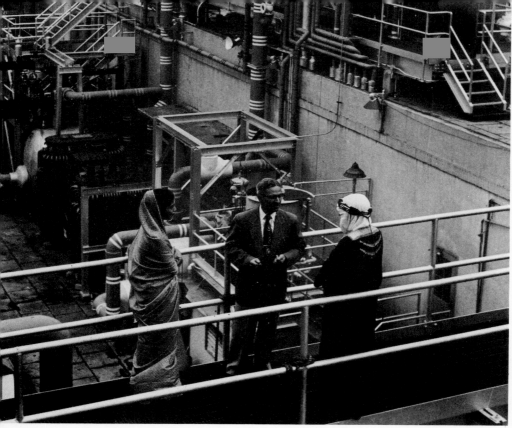

Puerto Rico News Service

Two visitors, interested in the ways in which Puerto Ricans have used scientific and industrial knowledge in their self-help program, observe one of the country's power plants.

represented with a few persons who went to Puerto Rico to study certain features of island life.

The project launched modestly as the Point Four Program is now included in the much larger program of the Administration for International Development. This agency, commonly called AID, operates as part of the United States Department of State.

Many of the trainees and observers who go to Puerto Rico are sent through agencies in the United States

Department of State. Others are sent through various agencies of the United Nations. Persons may be sent to Puerto Rico by their own governments, by colleges, or by private organizations. Some are invited to the island by the Puerto Rican government.

Observers carry on their activities under the guidance of the Office of Educational and Cultural Exchange, an agency of the Commonwealth Department of State. Opportunities are given the observers to see and to study educational and economic practices, and cultural features of Puerto Rico. Workshops and tours to study certain areas of life are scheduled from time to time.

The Technical Co-operation Program is directed by an agency of the Commonwealth Department of State. The help given to the trainee begins when he steps off the plane or boat. He is met by a representative of the agency, who aids him in finding a place to live. After the trainee is settled, he attends a lecture about Puerto Rico, and has the opportunity afterward to ask questions and discuss island life.

The trainee's next step is usually to talk with a training officer about the program he wishes to follow. The officer places him where he can receive the training he requests. The trainee then sets to work to acquire new facts and skills. His training may require a few days, a few weeks, or a few months. Some trainees have stayed in the island for a year.

The technique which the trainee wishes to learn determines where he will work. Those trainees who want to learn about industrial development are assigned to *Fomento*. This agency places the trainees in plants, banks, or other places where they can best be trained. In a similar way, trainees may be sent to other agencies of government, to business concerns, or to the colleges on the island, to receive specific training. All gladly work with the Technical Program, for they are proud of Puerto Rico's part in sharing the keys to progress.

There is scarcely a feature of Puerto Rican life that has not been studied by some foreign visitor to the island. But certain areas command more attention than others. Among the more popular areas are *Fomento*'s program for industrial development, self-help housing, vocational education, community education, the public health program, and government administration.

In addition to trainees and observers working on short-term assignments, there are foreign students studying in Puerto Rico. All of the island's colleges have such students, who are regularly enrolled for the full college year.

International Exchange

International exchange works two ways. Far more people go to Puerto Rico for training and observation than go away from the island, but some Puerto Ricans do go abroad to study or to aid other nations. The Organization of American States, made up of nations in the Western Hemisphere, has a scholarship program. Puerto Ricans, supported by OAS scholarships, are studying in certain Latin American countries. Puerto Ricans also share in the scholarship program of the United Nations and of some other organizations. Brief exchange visits of high-school students of Puerto Rico and certain other countries are now in operation. Many Puerto Ricans have gone to other nations to teach new techniques or to advise on plans for development.

During World War II, the United States, Great Britain, France, and the Netherlands formed a loose organization through which they cooperated in the Caribbean area. At that time all of these nations had island colonies in the Caribbean. Since most of the colonies have now achieved self-government, the former organization has given place to a new one.

The Caribbean Organization unites the self-governing islands in working together to reach further solutions of their problems. The Caribbean Organization has established its headquarters, called the Caribbean Center, in San Juan. The Center, with an excellent library, will draw more students of Caribbean problems to Puerto Rico.

In the hills near Arecibo is the Peace Corps' Rio Abajo camp. Groups of Americans serving in the Peace Corps come to the camp for periods of training.

The Peace Corps was established in 1961 by action of the Congress of the United States. The Corps enlists American men and women who will teach the skills needed by the people of underdeveloped countries. Each member of the Peace Corps is required to take a period of training for the work he is to do. The Corps members at Rio Abajo camp practice rugged physical exercises and language skills, and gain experience in the type of work they will do when assigned to a country for service. For example, some of them train with the Community Education workers so that later, in rural communities in other countries, they may help people solve their own community problems.

Recently the University of Puerto Rico, Inter-American

University, and Catholic University signed an agreement with the head of the Peace Corps. Under this agreement, the three universities will provide instruction for Corps members assigned to certain types of activities.

The coming of the Peace Corps to Puerto Rico was another forward step in the island's program of service to the world. The Puerto Ricans are writing a record for all men to read. It is the record of a people who, having lifted themselves out of misery, are now extending a helping hand to those who still suffer deep distress.

[20]

Goal for the Future

Governor Luis Muñoz Marín made a speech at Harvard University on Commencement Day in 1955. In that speech, Governor Muñoz stated a new goal for Puerto Rico. The Governor said, "In the Declaration of Independence of the United States, the young Republic was dedicated to the rights of life, liberty, and the pursuit of happiness. In Puerto Rico we are trying to bring to success Operation Bootstrap . . . the right to life; Operation Commonwealth . . . the right to liberty; and Operation Serenity . . . the pursuit of happiness."

Operation Serenity

Operation Bootstrap and Operation Commonwealth were accepted programs before 1955. Operation Serenity was proposed by the Governor as a new goal. In the years since 1955, it has become an important goal for Puerto Rico.

What did Governor Muñoz mean by Operation Serenity? What are the Puerto Rican people doing to achieve this goal?

Operation Bootstrap was an effort to provide jobs that would make it possible for Puerto Ricans to earn decent livings. Operation Commonwealth was a plan that gave Puerto Ricans political freedom and self-government. Operation Serenity was proposed as a program to help the Puerto Ricans use the money they earn and the freedom they enjoy to build lives that would bring them inner peace and satisfaction.

Operation Serenity is based upon the idea that the possessions that can be bought with money will not alone make people happy. Governor Muñoz has again and again expressed the hope that the Puerto Ricans will use their possessions as means to greater happiness, not as ends in themselves.

The idea which Operation Serenity presents is not new to the Puerto Ricans. It is a very ancient and important truth. The idea is stated in the Bible in the words, "Man does not live by bread alone." But its use as a stated goal for a modern government is new. In 1960, the Popular Democratic Party presented Operation Serenity as a program supported by the party. The voters gave the party a victory in the 1960 election, and by their votes accepted Operation Serenity as a goal for the future.

The government of Puerto Rico is promoting the program of serenity in various ways. One method is through education, which will prepare people to understand their culture. Another is through programs that help people to create new forms of art and learning. The government uses its agencies concerned with planning to make certain that people may have opportunities to develop satisfying lives. Puerto Ricans find fun and recreation in parks, playgrounds, public beaches, athletic fields, camps, and picnic areas. They enjoy plays, concerts, ballets, art exhibits, and books provided by public libraries.

The Puerto Ricans are putting into practice Governor Muñoz's belief that the economy of a country should be "the servant of the people's culture and not the master." The income that expanding industry and business produce is used to secure services and opportunities that help their people live better lives.

Important Plebiscite

The Puerto Rican people are preparing to make an important decision that will affect all their future thereafter. On July 25, 1962, the tenth anniversary of the Commonwealth, Governor Muñoz announced that a plebiscite, or voting, would be held within a few months to allow Puerto Ricans to indicate their wishes about the future permanent status of the island. In the plebiscite the voters would choose among a broadened Commonwealth, full independence, or statehood.

In a later radio broadcast to the people, Governor Muñoz, who favors a "more perfect Commonwealth" on a permanent basis, said that such a status would "fix the permanence . . . of the union between Puerto Rico and the United States; increase the liberty and authority of our people over their own affairs; define the authority which it is necessary to delegate to the Government of the United States . . . and create a means of participation of our people in the exercise of the authority of the Federal Government in matters which affect Puerto Rico."

The Governor is convinced that either independence or statehood would bring economic ruin to the island. He believes that either status would cause an increase in taxes, the loss of revenue now received from certain duties collected by the federal government but given to Puerto Rico, and possibly the loss of industry attracted to the island because Puerto Ricans pay no federal income taxes.

The Statehood Republican Party does not agree with the Governor. Leaders of the Party argue that statehood would cause more industries to come to Puerto Rico and thus insure a bright future. But they place the question of status above the economic issue. Luis Ferré, stating the Party's view, said, "Only federated statehood will place Puerto Rico in a situation of dignity and equality with the rest of the union. We are American citizens."

The Governor's proposal for a plebiscite to be held within a few months was strongly opposed by the Statehood Republican Party. Although the Party wants to achieve statehood, it does not consider that this could be accomplished quickly. This point of view was stated by the president of the Party, Senator Miguel Angel Garcia Mendéz, when he said, "the Congress of the United States is not yet ready to grant statehood." The Statehood Republican Party also opposed the plebiscite because it did not find the three choices announced by Governor Muñoz satisfactory. The Party argued that if a plebiscite were held it should offer a choice only between independence and statehood.

Those Puerto Ricans who favor independence had not asked for an immediate plebiscite, but their basic position is that they are willing, for the sake of independence, to give up the great economic and political advantage that Puerto Rico enjoys by its association with the United States. They do not think any price is too great to pay for gaining the position of a fully independent nation.

The proposal to hold a plebiscite aroused spirited discussion, both in the Puerto Rican Legislature and among the people of the island. After the issue had been debated for some weeks the Commonwealth Legislature agreed upon a plan of action. On November 21, 1962, the legislature approved, by a very large majority, a resolution providing that the executive branch of the Puerto Rican government shall negotiate with the Congress of the United States improvements in the Commonwealth form of government. The resolution provided further that when such negotiations have been concluded a plebiscite shall be held which will offer the voters a choice among the improved Commonwealth, statehood, and independence.

Governor Muñoz believes that there is need for Congress to define more specifically both Puerto Rico's powers over its own affairs and the powers of the federal government in those matters that are essential for carrying out federal functions. He would like to secure greater participation of Puerto Ricans in national affairs that affect Puerto Rico, as for example in voting for the President and Vice-President of the United States. The Governor believes that, since Puerto Ricans pay no federal income tax, a plan should be worked out by which Puerto Rico makes some payment to the treasury of the United States. These and other proposals will be laid before Congress and will probably be settled only after many months of debate and public discussion.

No date has been fixed for the plebiscite, and none can be fixed until Congress acts upon the proposals for an improved Commonwealth. While the Governor works to secure a permanent union with the United States, the Statehood Republican Party will seek to increase the sentiment for statehood, and those who favor independence will try to advance their cause. The will of the Puerto Rican people in the matter will be expressed when the plebiscite is held.

If the vote of the people should favor either statehood or independence the next decision must be made by the Congress of the United States. Only Congress has the power to grant statehood or independence. Since the provisions for an improved Commonwealth will have been agreed upon before the plebiscite, a vote favoring the Commonwealth will cement the permanent union between Puerto Rico and the United States.

Two-Way Benefits

Puerto Rico has benefited from its association with the United States. The democratic ideals and the pattern of organization used in its government came largely from the United States. Puerto Rican goods are shipped into the States without the payment of import taxes. Neither the Puerto Rican people, nor companies operating in Puerto Rico, pay income taxes to the federal government; and this provision has favored the development of industry in the island. Taxes collected in the States on Puerto Rican rum are turned back to the island. The Commonwealth

President John F. Kennedy was the guest of Governor Luis Muñoz Marín at La Fortaleza in 1961, at which time the two leaders discussed problems of mutual concern.

shares in money appropriated by the Congress of the United States to pay for special services to the people. Such funds have helped in the island to pay for school lunches, build roads and hospitals, secure loans for home-owners, support vocational schools, and provide a variety of other services.

The United States has received certain advantages from its relationship with Puerto Rico. One is its trade with the island. In 1961–1962, Puerto Rico imported eight hundred million dollars' worth of goods from the States.

Puerto Rico has created better understanding of the United States in Latin America, where differences in language, economic conditions, and ways of living had caused lack of understanding. Many Latin Americans receiving training in Puerto Rico, while learning new ways of work, have the opportunity to observe the benefits that the island has gained from its association with the United

States. Puerto Ricans are Latin Americans, but many of them are equally at home in North America. Leaders such as Governor Muñoz, with understanding of both areas, are helping to strengthen the ties between North Americans and Latin Americans.

The Bridge to Freedom

Puerto Rico has contributed to the solution of world problems. It has shown that a poverty-stricken land can overcome its poverty; that people without hope can learn to meet their own needs. It is the world's best laboratory for training citizens from underdeveloped countries in techniques necessary for advancement. It has created a new form of government, under which a small, poor country can be associated with a large, rich country to the advantage of both. It has proved that an underdeveloped country can change into a well-developed country within the framework of a democratic government.

Puerto Rico has built a bridge to freedom. It is a bridge from an old way of life to a new way; a bridge from the sorrows endured under colonialism to the joys realized through self-government. It is a bridge over which the Puerto Ricans have moved to the new opportunities and new goals that freedom provides.

A businessman from the United States, living in Ponce, said that Puerto Rico is "as close to paradise as man will ever see." A balmy climate, pleasant scenes, and a kindly people living in modest comfort and enjoying cultural advantages in the clean, pure air of freedom, do, indeed, make a place that is "close to paradise"!

Pronunciation Guide

PROPER NOUNS

Alegría, Ricardo	Ah-lay-gree'-ah, Ree-kahr'-do
Almeida	Ahl-may'-da
Alonso, Manuel A.	Ah-lohn'-so, Mahn-wel' Ah.
Anteneo Puertorriqueño	Ahn-tay-nay'-o Pwair-to-ree-kayn'-yo
Arawak	Ah'-rah-wahk
Arecibo	Ah-ray-see'-bo
Astol, Felix	Ahs-tohl', Fay-lees'
Benítez, Jaime	Bay-nee'-tess, Hy'-may
Borinquén	Bo-reen-ken'
Caguas	Kah'-gwahs
Caja de Muertos	Kah'-hah day Mwair'-tos
Campeche, José	Kahm-pay'-chay, Ho-say'
Campos, Pedro Albizu	Kahm'-pohs, Pay'-dro Ahl-bee'-su
Caparra	Kah-pah'-rah
Caribbean	Kari-be'-an
Caribs	Kah'-ribs
Carrión, Arturo Morales	Kah-ree-ohn', Ahr-too'-ro Moh-rah'-lays
Casa Blanca	Kah'-sah Blahn'-cah
Cepeda, Orlando	Say-pay'-da, Ohr-lahn'-do

Clemente, Roberto	Klay-men'-tay, Roh-bair'-to
Cofresí, Roberto	Kah-fray-see', Roh-bair'-to
Collado, Ramón	Kol-yah'-do, Rah-mon'
Cortes	Kor'-tace
Culebra	Koo-lay'-brah
El Cañuelo	El Kah-new-áy-lo
El Comandante	El Ko-mahn-dahn'-tay
El Fanguito	El Fahn-ghee'-to
El Morro	El Mor'-ro
El Yunque	El Yoon'-kay
Escambrón	Ace-kahm-brohn'
Ferré, Luis	Fay-ray', Loo-ees'
Fomento	Fo-main'-to
Gautier, Felisa Rincón de	Goh-tee-ay', Fay-lee'-sah Reen-kohn' day
Gerónimo	Hay-ro'-nee-mo
Giralt, Ramón Power y	Hee-rahlt', Rah-mohn' Po-wáir ee
Guánica	Gwah'-nee-kah
Isern, Antonio Fernos	Ee-sairn', Ahn-tohn'-yo Fair'-nos
La Casa del Libro	Lah Kah'-sah del Lee'-bro
La Fortaleza	Lah For-tah-lay'-sah
La Perla	Lah Pair'-lah
Loíza Aldea	Loh-ee'-sah Ahl-day'-ah
Mayagüez	Mah-yah-gwa'ce
Moscoso, Teodoro	Mohs-koh'-so, Tay-o-doh'-ro
Muñoz Marín, Luis	Moon-yoh's Mah-reen', Loo-ees'
Niña	Neen'-yah
Piñero, Jesús T.	Peen-yair'-oh, Hay-su's Tay.
Pinta	Peen'-tah
Ponce	Pohn'-say
Ponce de León	Pohn'-say day Lay-ohn'
Porta Coeli	Pohr'-tah Che'-lee
Pou, Miguel	Pooh, Mee-gail'
Puerto Rico	Pwair'-to Ree'-ko
Rio Abajo	Ree'-oh Ah-bah'-ho
Rio Piedras	Ree'-oh Pee-ay'-drahs
Rivera, Luis Muñoz	Ree-vay'-rah, Loo-ees' Moon-yoh's
San Antonio	Sahn Ahn-tohn'-yo
San Cristóbal	Sahn Crees-to'-bahl
San Germán	Sahn Hair-mahn'

San José	Sahn Ho-say'
San Juan	Sahn Whahn'
San Juan Bautista	Sahn Whahn' Bow-tees'-tah
San Juan de la Cruz	Sahn Whahn' day lah Croos'
Santa María	Sahn'-tah Mah-ree'-ah
Santurce	Sahn-toor'-say
Tío, Lola Rodríguez de	Tee'-oh, Loh'-lah Rod-ree'-gayce day
Vieques	Vee-ay'-kayce

SPANISH WORDS

acerola	ah-say-roh'-lah
agregado	ah-gray-gah'-do
aguinaldo	ah-ghee-nahl'-do
amajábanas	ah-mah-hah'-bah-nahs
arroz con dulce	ah-ros' kohn dool'-say
bohío	bo-ee'-o
búcare	boo'-kah-ray
central	sen-trahl'
coquí	ko-kee'
cuatro	kwah'-tro
danza	dahn'-sah
décima	day'-see-mah
doña	dohn'-yah
el niño y su mundo	el neen'-yo ee soo moon'-do
"Esta es su casa"	Ace'-tah ace soo cah'-sah
güicharo	gwee-chah'-ro
güiro	gwee'-ro
jíbaro	hee'-bah-ro
lechón asado	lay-chohn' ah-sah'-do
machete	mah-chay'-tay
majarete	mah-hah-ray'-tay
maraca	mah-rah'-kah
paso-fine	pah'-so-fee'-nay
pava	pah'-vah
plena	play'-nah
reinita	ray-nee'-tah
santero	sahn-tay'-ro
santos	sahn'-tos
zafra	sah'-frah

Index